P9-DCR-688

Walt Roth

11/16/16

waltroth2@gmail.com

TAKING RISKS

Getting Ahead in Business and Life

ALL RIGHTS RESERVED

No part of this publication may be reproduced, stored in a retrieval system, or transmitted in any form or by any means—electronic, mechanical, photocopying, or otherwise—without written permission.

Copyright © 2014 by Meadow Brook Farm Publishing LLC

First Editing Edition 2014

Meadow Brook Farm Publishing LLC, Waukesha Wisconsin

Publisher: Leon P. Janssen
Editor: Gene Medford
Designer: Working Class Publishing
Printer: Worzalla Publishing

ISBN-13   978-0-9822431-4-5
ISBN-10   0-9822431-4-6

Dedicated to
My Wife, Anne

Contents

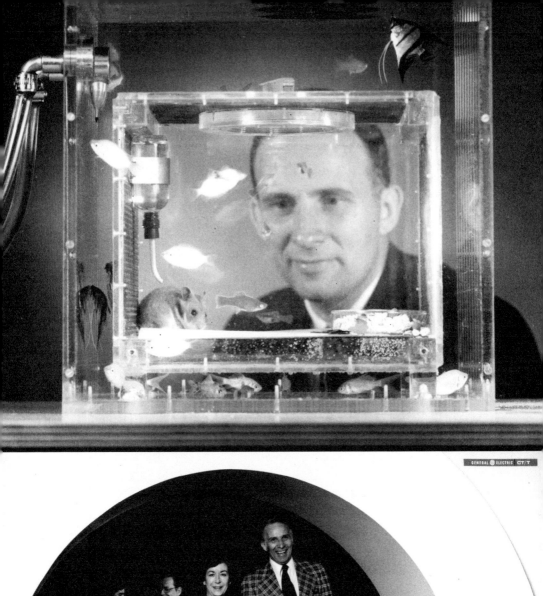

Introduction

THIS BOOK HAS TWO OBJECTIVES. The first is to encourage young people and corporate employees to be more entrepreneurial and willing to take reasonable risks in their educations, professional, and personal activities. The second objective has to do with corporations that have become too risk-averse.

I love the U.S. and I have always felt it was Number One in the world for developing new technology. While working for 42 years in a big corporation, namely General Electric, where I reported to CEO Jack Welch for 20 years, I saw entrepreneurship at its best. GE workers were encouraged to take risks, or as Jack said, "Take a swing," and most of the company's businesses became #1 or #2 in the world.

Now, I am growing concerned: U.S. corporations are becoming increasingly conservative; they are becoming dependent on buying or licensing new technologies, or acquiring the start-ups that invent new products. Even corporate research labs are so carefully managed that they are becoming risk-averse.

To make it worse, many successful start-ups are being acquired by overseas corporations. For example, in my present career as a director of multiple start-ups, my last two "cash-outs," both high-tech companies, were acquired by foreign corporations. This is being coupled with foreign companies, particularly those from China, increasing their scientific research efforts and even acquiring U.S. patents at a rate that will soon exceed U.S. firms. The production of solar panels, flat panel televisions, digital cameras, CT scanners, and too many other products to mention is moving offshore at an alarming rate.

The United States is losing what it once did best: nurturing new technologies and bringing them to market. Even when a technology was discovered overseas, the U.S. used to be capable of becoming the world producer of the product. Jet engines, CT scanners, and penicillin were invented overseas but, in each case, U.S. corporations developed the winning products and achieved dominant positions in world markets.

For example, the British company EMI invented a new x-ray imaging machine called computerized trans-axial tomography (the CT scanner). It could show tumors in the human brain for the first time. Though it took 4½ minutes per scan, no competition appeared for two years. Finally, a number of medical technology firms around the world recognized how significant a breakthrough this was (CT scanner sales would soon far exceed those of conventional x-ray machines). At one time, 15 companies began developing similar scanners, making incremental improvements on the original EMI technology. A two-minute scanner became the goal.

Two major corporate research labs invented scanners that could, in seconds, make images that were better than those the EMI machines needed minutes to create. One was a conservative overseas company that worked on the idea in its corporate research lab until business management concluded that it would take years to develop a viable product. Therefore, they decided the new technology was too risky to pursue and chose to concentrate on developing a 2-minute scanner instead.

The second company was General Electric. Having just been appointed by Jack Welch as the general manager of the GE X-Ray business, I was very excited about a breakthrough and took a huge risk in order that we might gain an advantage over our numerous competitors. As it happened, we successfully developed and commercialized a five-second fan-beam scanner. In three years,

GE won 50% of the U.S. CT market and, in five years, 50% of the world market. The GE fan-beam scanner became the "gold standard." Even in the early years, the business was profitable for GE, while the competition battled for survival. The small start-up companies soon fell by the wayside; only when the big companies copied the GE breakthrough did we have any real competition. We took a big risk and it made all the difference.

CT was not a unique experience. In this book, I intend to present other examples of how taking risks led to GE's greatest successes. Yes, we made acquisitions at times, but our internally nurtured inventions were always the most successful.

So what is the problem today? Simply that major U.S. corporations are becoming risk-averse. CEOs are so concerned with achieving quarterly estimates that they are reluctant to invest in new products and ideas with a long payback. They fear wasting money on research. Instead, buying a start-up with funds off the balance sheet saves the operating expense of research and early development dollars. With so much focus on quarterly profits, why not let start-ups bear the risk of sorting out the real breakthroughs?

Employees are also given short-term goals. They are stretched to the point where extra work hours are assumed when planning a program schedule. The days when companies would give their employees the right, even the obligation, to spend up to 15% of their time on new ideas is only a memory. Thinking "outside the box" is not encouraged, except in advertising. Extraneous reporting is too frequent. Staffing cutbacks discourage even good employees from taking the risk of "bootlegging" an experiment, a practice that was encouraged in the past.

The acquisition of start-ups by U.S. corporations has become all too common, even though the results have not been all that successful. Rarely is the technology as good as was expected; a corporate effort usually is required to clean up the problems found in the acquired prototypes. Failure of installed start-up products in the field is common. The problems customers experience are usually blamed on the parent corporation.

Worse yet, bright young entrepreneurs leaving college often prefer to work for start-ups. That's fine, but only one in ten of those companies will succeed. What a waste of time and talent. If only large, established businesses could acquire more of these eager, creative minds as they establish their careers.

The second objective of this book is to make young entrepreneurs more valuable to a potential employer. Even if you have joined a conservative company, I'll show you how taking worthwhile risks can help you positively impact your organization; how your contributions will separate you from your peers. And while you may not change the culture of the entire company at first, your impact will be felt beyond your own area of activity as you earn greater responsibilities. Like Jack Welch, you may gradually change a company's philosophy and even become its CEO.

CELEBRATING RISK

This book is about my experience being a risk-taker in a variety of situations: first, in a risk-accepting nuclear laboratory; and, second, at the end of my 42-year career, as director of a central research laboratory that, in spite of its charter, had not been as courageous as it might have been. Though it is my personal story, it includes many "higher-ups" who took a risk on me as I progressed through my professional career. Their support is what made all the difference.

It is based on my experience and shows how everyone in a corporation—from the newly hired college graduate to the CEO—can be an entrepreneur. Progressive U.S. corporations help the country maintain its industrial leadership. With cutting-edge products and processes, everyone wins—workers, consumers, and stockholders alike.

When I retired from General Electric, I was deeply satisfied with the career I had enjoyed while evolving from an individual contributor to my final position as the Senior Vice President of Research and Development (also known as the Chief Technology Officer in today's terminology). Very few chemical engineers have achieved the expertise that I acquired during my journey through so many challenging professional positions: an R & D manager, a venture manager, a general manager of three different GE organizations, including a materials department, a six-business materials division, and a group-level business in medical imaging.

Along the way, I progressed from having one technician reporting to me to more than 10,000 reportees in GE's worldwide medical business. As CTO, I supervised 450 Ph.Ds at GE's renowned research laboratory. Over the course of my GE career, I made inventions and earned patents for them, designed a plant, managed teams that made world-class breakthroughs, and nurtured a medical technology operation that became a $2 billion business. GE Healthcare has continued to thrive over the years and is a $17 billion enterprise today, still based on the strategy I implemented of working hand in hand with the Corporate R & D Center. I am extremely proud of my team that produced "gold standard" CT and MRI imaging technologies—tools for physicians around the world to provide better care for their patients. But it was not just in technology that we achieved significant results. Tactical improvements in marketing, sales, financing, and even in human resources were part of the strategy. Real business success requires all these elements in order to produce solid results, even from new ideas.

For a kid who grew up in a town of 850 people and graduated high school in a class of 25, only two of whom were boys going on with their schooling, the results were unexpected. I have never claimed to be the smartest or hardest worker, but I was blessed with good parents, wonderful teachers, and excellent mentors throughout my many experiences. Perhaps, most importantly, I reported to Jack Welch while he progressed from a GE division manager to CEO. I was gratified when he selected me for four different executive positions and tried to vindicate his confidence. Perhaps my achievements even helped Jack advance his own career and validate his mentorship.

One more GE example: during our development of magnetic resonance imaging, we noted that ultrasound scanners were also gaining prominence. We had been too busy with CT and MRI to also put a major homegrown effort into ultrasound, so we acquired a promising start-up in the field. It was a failure. We learned and started from scratch to develop a breakthrough digital ultrasound technology at the Research Laboratory. GE is now #1 in that key modality as well. That was the last time I looked to a start-up for a new technology.

I am so glad my senior management experience spanned the period 1971 to 1993, and that I was working for Jack Welch. He was an extraordinary entrepreneur who broke new ground, took risks right and left, and gave credit to employees for "taking a swing." His impact on my career is detailed in the chapters that follow.

Did Jack expect performance? Absolutely. And, yes, I missed a few budgets, but recovered the next quarter. At the heart of our relationship was the fact that I gave Jack very few surprises and we worked as a team.

Since retiring in 1993, I have thought about what made my business experience so fulfilling. It was achieved while having a balanced family life; with my wife's unbelievable dedication and support, we raised three sons who are making their own marks in the world. My wildest daydreams about my future career while delivering newspapers in my early teens were far surpassed.

Now, when I work with young people, they often ask what made my career so successful. I have distilled my answer to four observations:

1. I tried to always do more than was required.

2. I was curious about every aspect of the business I was in.

3. I liked to think "outside the box" and did not hesitate to offer new ideas.

4. I took risks. I was not afraid to fail, though I hated to have it happen. I do not subscribe to "win through failing" and dislike articles that encourage that philosophy. Learning that something didn't work was a valuable lesson, but it was never my intent to fail in a task.

Of these personal factors, the first three are generally accepted in business and in life. It is the fourth that is losing favor in Corporate America and my reason for this book.

Yes, there have been many books written on taking risks, but most apply to start-ups. This one is specifically directed towards taking risks in major enterprises—"intrapreneurship," if you will. Of course, there are some large companies, especially in the computer and software arenas, that are a combination of a start-up and large corporation. They don't need this book. Rather, it is specifically directed to the bulk of corporations that have become "fat and happy" with too much gradual growth through incremental improvements or acquiring start-ups. The United States deserves more.

During my last 20 years with the company, I was mentored and promoted by GE's peerless CEO, Jack Welch, For the final 6 years as CTO, I sat on his side of the executive table as we reviewed the strategies and budgets of all the individual segments of the GE structure. So, in addition to my own business management, I was an observer and contributor to the plans of multiple GE businesses and saw firsthand the benefits of taking risks.

At age 65, I "retired" and started investing my GE earnings in 20 start-up companies, serving on the boards of 10, and never being bashful about challenging the management of them all. This has been more fun and profitable for me than playing golf or fishing. Most importantly, it has given me an excellent understanding about the challenges faced by high-tech start-ups.

I have observed the lengthy time and cost of commercializing a new technology in a private company, in contrast to what can be accomplished by the same founder/inventor as part of a larger entrepreneurial company. I grieve that the time and talent of so many exceptional people are being diverted from entrepreneurial goals. Too often, I have seen CEOs or founders spending over half their time raising money, a distraction I never had at GE. Similarly, many entrepreneurial CTOs don't have the equipment or specialized instruments they need, rarely a problem in large corporations. The more I see start-ups struggle to succeed, the more I understand why so many of our entrepreneurs are only 50% effective. The country is not benefiting from this trend.

In the past several years, I have been co-teaching a course on "leadership" at a graduate college. Most of the students want to be entrepreneurs and assume that means a risky start-up with a huge opportunity. Certainly, we need startups, but we also need our major companies to be developing new products and businesses for their continued global successes. We need entrepreneurs wanting to join corporations, and corporations wanting to hire entrepreneurs.

This book is aimed at a variety of readers, from CEOs to young people and their parents. No one may find every chapter applicable. For parents of young boys and girls, the first chapter may be most important. For CEOs, the later chapters describing my observations as general manager and chief technology officer may be most useful in helping develop entrepreneurial cultures in their companies. The middle chapters are valuable for all readers.

Let's look at each category of readers in more detail:

1. For managers at all levels of any enterprise, from a program manager to a general manager to a senior vice president, an entrepreneurial attitude will help bring clarity and boldness to your decisions. Even if you work for a conservative, risk-averse manager, following these suggestions will increase the likelihood that YOU will become his or her successor!

2. To new employees, individual contributors, and first-level managers, my experiences will give examples of how being more entrepreneurial can get you off to a better start in any organization.

3. To college students, being entrepreneurial can improve your resumes and increase your chances of getting hired. What you do in college that can be added to your resume will affect your getting interviews with the companies you choose.

4. To high school students, you could do worse than read this book, especially the chapters on my high school and college experiences. I'm not optimistic that many students will take the time required, so I also recommend the book to parents. I was fortunate to have parents that did not complain if I blew a few fuses

while learning how to be a clever electrician. Parents can stifle or encourage entrepreneurial habits. In fact, the chapter for high school students is really for grandparents as much as parents. It will refresh your memory about your own experiences. As a bonus, your grandchildren will love to hear your stories.

5. To college professors and graduate school instructors, this text might sharpen your academic skills and increase your impact on your students. Of course, colleges are also businesses, so the chapter on my own college experience could be enlightening for deans and presidents.

6. To all, this book should make you smile. It is a true story about a very lucky individual who is now the father of three entrepreneurial sons who are doing well, though not one is in a corporation. They all had to do their own thing.

I wish I had read this book when I was a parent with children at home. Hopefully, our five granddaughters will read it. I believe that taking risks can be practiced by all, no matter the gender, color, origin, or financial status. It costs nothing extra to become an entrepreneur, and doing so will insure your having more impact on society, a more exciting career, and more money in your pocket or to give away. Your parents, your spouse, and your children will be proud of what you accomplished.

In conclusion, I hope it is not necessary to point out that risk-taking can be carried to extremes, as demonstrated by racecar drivers, gamblers, political extremists, and many others. The risks I will discuss were legal, possible to accomplish, and worth the effort to achieve. Both the potential results and the cost of failure need to be understood, as well as the realization that no one can expect to be successful 100% of the time.

1939

Prologue

IT MAY SEEM STRANGE to start a book on taking risks by discussing activities during my school period. I believe, however, what happened in those 18 years of studies equipped and inspired me to be more entrepreneurial in business. But this is not just about me. It is about my parents, teachers, and employers. The latter were important because, in multiple cases, they heard a brash kid ask for a paying job and rewarded him with the opportunity to prove himself.

Entrepreneurial genes, or order of birth, are sometimes thought to be the key, but I believe the environment is more important. Perhaps that is where parents and order of birth have a connection. I remember a teacher who told my high school freshman class that everyone could excel in something. I was upset that he had no hope for me in athletics, farming, or construction, where he believed most of my friends could excel. But from day one, he said I could excel in science, which at that time did not sound too exciting. What he should have said, in addition, is that everyone could be an entrepreneur in their area of excellence. It is unfortunate that not enough emphasis is given to that aspect of each person's career.

So this chapter is dedicated to encouragement of "kids" of any age to be entrepreneurs in what they do best. If it is playing a guitar, be proficient but also be different; establish a style and presence; advance the art; create an impact. Students learning to be farmers should also be trained to work on continuous improvement in both product and productivity. They should not be content with farming the same ways as their fathers and grandfathers. It all comes back to taking risks. Fortunately, my teachers and parents instilled in me the desire to have a positive impact on my school, my family, my friends, and myself. Without knowing it, I was becoming an entrepreneur.

I hope you will quickly read through the next two chapters about my school years or, if you wish, skip directly to Chapter 3 where my professional experience begins.

Enough! It is time for you to see how this worked out.

Chapter 1

Taking Risks During My Early Years

I LAUNCHED MY FIRST BUSINESS venture at the age of eight with my best friend, Junior Rapp. We lived in New Bloomfield, Pa., a town of 850 people north of Harrisburg. It was 1936, and we both received a weekly allowance of 15 cents. My parents required me to tithe one nickel to the Sunday school collection basket, and save another for big expenditures, such as a new baseball glove. The remaining nickel would just cover the cost of a coveted ice cream cone.

So Junior and I took a small risk by setting up a roadside lemonade business. My mother agreed to make cookies and his mother made the lemonade, which certainly reduced our risk.

I also knew that Junior had taken tap dance lessons and could play a trumpet—he could actually do both simultaneously. We set up a stage on his lawn next to a card table; he would perform for customers while I made change. But there turned out to be an unexpected risk when some girls established their own lemonade venture down the street and waited for us to fail. The competition excited us all. Win or lose, both teams got excellent experience.

My next venture in taking risks was mowing lawns—a huge increase in pay but hard work. It was not a big-risk enterprise since I had very little competition. I learned to knock on doors and ask for the job, which taught me to accept "no" at an early age. I also learned to charge by the hour, not for the job, after one woman insisted I cut her lawn both north-south and east-west.

Across the street from our home lived an elderly widow, who was a very young girl during the Civil War. She remembered the sound of cannons coming from Carlisle, Pa., which was the farthest north the Confederate Army ever got. She wanted me to cut and trim her lawn to very precise specifications. Working as fast as I could, it took me one hour of hard labor to accomplish this for which she gave me 8¢ for the effort! When I told my mother what had happened, she had no sympathy and suggested a little bit of charity would be good for my soul. Six years later, I submitted an essay to a county high school competition on the subject of "How did the Civil War impact Perry County?" I embellished the story the lady had told me about hearing the cannon fire 15 miles away, and of Carlisle natives coming over Sterret's Gap in case General Lee was victorious at Gettysburg. I won the contest, which was worth $20. As mother told me, "You never know when a good turn will be rewarded."

MORE YOUTHFUL LESSONS

By the time I was 12, I was a newspaper delivery boy for the *Harrisburg Evening News*. Among my peers, I was the one who asked for the job. It is interesting how that has paid off for me time and again. I started out only having 18 papers to deliver each night. It was hardly worth the effort, but it was a risk I took to get started. Before long, the older boy I worked for retired and I inherited his 80-customer paper route. Not only was I now delivering papers, but I also was responsible for signing up new subscribers and collecting 15¢ from each of my 100+ subscribers every Saturday. Now I had to worry about deadbeats who'd try to "stick" me. Only once did I ever appeal to my father to help me collect what had run up to be a $1.50 bill. I promised myself that I would not let that happen again.

Eventually, I acquired the town's morning route as well. Because I was willing to take the risk of nurturing an 18-paper route, I ended up with a much bigger enterprise.

By the time I was 15, my old buddy, Junior, landed a job at the A & P grocery store in town. Not to be outdone, I wanted the prize summer job offered at Weis, our other grocery store. I marched in and told the manager how interested I was and what a great benefit I would be to his staff. I got the job and started out stocking shelves. The third day on the job found me lifting two-pound boxes of Saltines to a top shelf, when one slipped, knocking a weight scale off the shelf and breaking it. No one saw it happen and for a second I wanted to hide the accident. Instead, I went to the store manager's office and told him what had happened. Shortly after, he promoted me to a part-time clerk. My responsible behavior convinced him to take the risk of letting me handle money.

Junior and I worked the same hours—half days during the week and from 8 a.m. until 11 p.m. on Saturdays. At the end of our long Saturday shifts, we'd get off work dead tired, but still with enough energy to go to the ice cream stand and split a pint of Hershey's ice cream. We would soon be joined by another buddy who had worked all day at the town's drug store. All three of us felt we had the best summer jobs available—all because we asked store managers for jobs that were never advertised.

World War II presented major opportunities for young people. Shortly after D-Day, I found out that heavy laborer jobs at the Middletown Army Air Depot paid $1 an hour plus overtime for Saturdays. This was real money! I didn't quite qualify physically— you had to weigh 130 pounds to be classified as a heavy laborer. So on the way to the initial weigh-in, I took several pounds of bananas with me and ate them on the long bus ride. I made the weight and got the job. My risk-attempt paid off by one pound.

Commuting to the depot was a chore. The bus left New Bloomfield at 5 a.m. and took an hour and a half to get to Middletown. So I was gone 12 hours a day, Monday through Saturday, and I still mowed some lawns after supper. But it was worth it. We were packing parts for the B-26s in Europe. It was a stirring experience during a rare time in our country. There were other high school kids also working there, and we worked hard because we felt we were doing what we could to help the war effort. Even my parents were impressed that I always made the 5 a.m. bus (with one exception).

By the time that summer was over I had saved $1,000. I bought a watch for myself and a good pen for my mother, who would wake up early every morning to see me off. You can calibrate those numbers to current dollars by comparing the cost of postage stamps: 3¢ then versus 49¢ cents today. I wonder how many kids today have saved $16,000 by the time they are ready for college.

To give any impression that I was missing out on fun with all these jobs is dead wrong. I had a lot of friends and we had our share of adventures and misadventures. I was an active Boy Scout, dabbled in photography with a darkroom that I put together in a home closet, learned to drive as soon as I was 16, and tried going out for sports (which I soon realized were not my calling). To get to the "away" games, I became the baseball manager and had to give the game summary to the Harrisburg newspaper after each event. I decided to become a sports announcer with Bill Stern as my hero, performing in amateur shows announcing make-believe games involving all my classmates with my imaginary microphone.

Clearly, I had great parents. My mother was a grade school teacher until she married my father, a teacher and high school principal, as well as an insurance agent carrying all the types of insurance that a local farming area could possibly want. They appreciated my dedication and energy and contributed in various ways. They got me my own toolbox early on, with which my buddies and I made Soapbox Derby racers, scooters, and our one disappointment—a boat that simply wouldn't float. I also made a light box for printing photographs. And if I blew a fuse in the house circuit once in awhile, my parents did not get upset, but figured that was just a part of my ongoing education.

I was frequently the leader of my band of friends, investigating one thing or another. One example was the "Stardust Circus" which I organized in our backyard. I rounded up all my friends who could do any sort of "trick" and put them in the show. The tricks were pretty lame, such as my girlfriend's dog that, on command, would go stand in a corner as if he were being punished. One fellow imitated walking a tight-wire by walking the length of a 2 x 4 placed on edge from one trestle to another. I "performed" on a trapeze, jumping from a box to catch the flying trapeze a whole four feet above the ground. "Stardust" was so bad that my mother was embarrassed that the kids had to pay 10¢ each to attend. She insisted on serving lemonade and cookies to justify the price.

REALLY IMPORTANT INFLUENCERS

Learning to be a leader or an entrepreneur can start at any age, but it certainly is helpful when parents and teachers go beyond the norm to provide you with opportunities to lead.

My favorite high school teacher was Coach Weigle. He taught American history, freshman science, sophomore biology, and, alternatively, chemistry and physics to the combined junior-senior class. He also coached football, basketball, and baseball. Though he soon saw that I didn't have much skill in sports, he thankfully invited me as a freshman to be his technical assistant in the science classes, setting up experiments in front of his classroom, keeping the solutions fresh in the basement laboratory, and putting things away in the storage closet, which was a treasure of all kinds of interesting gadgets. At Christmas time one year, he received a 2-inch thick catalog from Edmund Scientific that had every scientific teaching item imaginable. He invited me to see what he could buy for $100, which is how our school got an electric eye that could be connected to do many things, including demonstrating the principles of photo emission and electronics to the physics class. I was soon setting up tricks, such as lighting up a room when people walked in—an amazing phenomenon in the early 1940s.

By my senior year I had decided that chemical engineering was the career for me. It combined chemistry and mathematics, two subjects in which I was very confident. Then I heard about a countywide American Legion contest that would award one $400 scholarship for the winner to attend a state college. All you had to do was write an essay on what you wanted to become after college. I honestly did not know how to make chemical engineering sound very exciting to the lay judges, all of whom were female English teachers in the local schools. I finally decided to write my essay on becoming an audio engineer, designing cathedrals and symphony halls—things I thought lay people could readily appreciate. It worked and I won the $400 scholarship, which paid half of my tuition for eight semesters at Penn State. Sometimes I feel guilty for taking that risk, but I actually found this area of technical architecture pretty interesting and, for one afternoon, I imagined this would be my career.

My dad was supportive of everything I undertook. When I had succeeded in saving $1,000 for college, he matched it and said "Let's see how far that will go."

We were both concerned that our small high school might not have prepared me quite as well for the chemical engineering curriculum at Penn State as the students coming from the big high schools in Harrisburg and other cities. So, to help me get ready, he asked a chemistry teacher at a nearby military academy to give me a two-week cram course following high school graduation. I was to leave for my first semester at Penn State in the middle of June. This teacher had a college freshman workbook and during those two intervening weeks we went through it for an hour or two every day, followed by another hour or so of homework in the evening. At the end, I took a college freshman "final exam" that he had and scored 95. That gave me great confidence as I began the coursework at Penn State.

I have to give credit to my high school principal, Mr. Melvin Paul, who did something that proved to be useful to me 25 years later. He intervened when I was goofing off and turned what could have become a punishment into an opportunity. That was during my senior year of high school when I had one hour of study hall every day that didn't require my time to finish my homework assignments. So, with another of my buddies, Fred Purdy, my competitor to be the top graduate and who then went to the University of Pittsburgh, we became pretty disruptive in study hall. Our innocent shenanigans caught the attention of Mr. Paul who called me in and said, "Penn State has a list of correspondence courses. We'd like you to pick one and the school will pay for it. Hopefully, it will keep you busy during study hall."

I picked radio technology, a subject that had always fascinated me. The workbook had pages to be completed and sent back to Penn State every Friday afternoon. By the following Friday, the assignments would come back corrected with appropriate notations of where I was wrong. It was wonderful. I built a crystal radio but couldn't pick up the nearest station, which was in Harrisburg. So, I took the bus into town one Saturday and went to a park where I could see the antenna on top of a hotel. I strung up a wire antenna between the benches and, yes, I was able to pick up the station. That's all I needed to know: it worked and I was thrilled! Since it was wartime, a policeman soon came by and made me wind up my antenna. Thirty-five years later, this course paid off as I began learning how MRI scanners work.

In my career as a corporate risk-taker and entrepreneur, I've often thought about the important values my parents instilled in me without ever saying a word. It goes right back to that lemonade stand I started when I was eight years old. My parents never made it too easy for me, or too hard. That 15-cent allowance gave me just enough after the obligatory tithing and saving to buy an ice cream. If they had not given me anything, then I might have done what some other kids were doing and stolen candy. Parents have a tremendous responsibility to make it neither too easy nor too hard.

Another satisfaction that came with the allowance was that it was earned. This is another important influence that parents can exert, instilling a pride of ownership in children. In our family, we were expected to do normal household chores that kids should be responsible for, like keeping our rooms in reasonable order. I also realized that the family just worked better if everyone did the little jobs they were assigned. It was always understood that we got the allowance because we were pulling our weight.

On a lighter note, I'll offer one more caution to parents. When it comes to buying "educational" toys for your kids, forget the kits. Kits make things too easy for the kids, and are not nearly as much fun. The things that came with my chemistry set were non-toxic, non-flammable, and didn't make very exciting experiments. We had a lot more fun when we discovered calcium carbide, a chemical that could be bought at the local hardware store for as little as 25¢. This is what goes into a miner's lamp. It reacts with water (or saliva) to make acetylene. If you have a can with a lid that is pressed on tight, some carbide, spit, and a hole in the bottom to ignite the acetylene, you have a firecracker that costs very little and can be recharged and set off hundreds of times.

Now, I know that working with such dangerous substances is risky, just like building a tree house. But that is how young people learn to evaluate what is a reasonable risk. Worse than not taking risks is being unable to evaluate the consequences, which is what growing up is supposed to be all about.

A FEW CONCLUSIONS

FOR STUDENTS: In grade school, you are exposed to many different subjects in class and in extracurricular activities. By 7th or 8th grade, it is valuable to select a couple of areas in which you can excel. For me, it was mathematics, playing the clarinet, and public speaking. To be an entrepreneur it helps to become proficient in a few areas. These areas can always change, but at least you begin thinking about your life's profession. In my case, science and mathematics grew in interest. And though a clarinet was fun to play, I realized I would never be that proficient.

In addition to schooling and play, you should have some time for "doing chores." If you are not asked by your parents, volunteer to do at least one activity around your home that requires daily, or at least weekly, effort. It could be making your bed, feeding the dog, mowing the lawn, or some such. Then be certain to make this a routine that does not require that your parents remind you. Demonstrate that you can perform a regular task responsibly.

Even if your allowance covers all of your needs and, hopefully, gives you some money for charity and a savings account, it is still advisable that at least by your high school junior year, you find a part-time job. Having a job outside of home demonstrates that you can be a dependable, happy, creative worker. It is valuable, not only for the extra cash you will earn, but also for the experience of selling yourself, pricing your service, and collecting the revenue due you. Babysitting, delivering papers, clerking in a store, or performing an entertaining skill are only a few of the activities from which you might choose.

Getting accepted by the college of your choice can be very competitive. All the activities listed will help on your *curriculum vitae* to the college application center. But what will you have that marks you as a leader, an innovator, an entrepreneur? Have you volunteered to help in a community activity? Have you joined a church club, band, Scouting group, Junior Achievement? It is better to be a leader in one of these than just a member in numerous groups.

Can you list one project that you initiated and saw through to completion that made the world a little better place?

FOR PARENTS: First of all, look through the possible activities listed for your children in the previous section. Help them find the areas where they can excel. Assist them in finding ways to be opportunistic in those areas. Help them find the joy in doing something really well. Compliment them for every achievement.

Give each of your kids a chance. All children need to have the experience of being pioneers, whether they're the first-born or the youngest. Middle and younger children need opportunities to be first, too. Help them to "think outside the box," not just follow or match the efforts of an elder sibling.

Give each of them challenges and expect some mistakes. It's part of learning to "take a swing." Taking a reasonable risk encourages stretching. Check their judgment in deciding what is a reasonable risk.

If your child gets a regular job, ask what the work rules are. Do all you can to help your child keep these rules. Periodically ask their employer how they are doing. Lastly, monitor how you child is being paid and how the money is being used. Is the proper tax withholding being made?

With your help, a job, and the financial and emotional rewards that come with it, is a wonderful learning opportunity for the child.

Until your children have become wage earners, remunerate them with an allowance. It's OK for doing chores around the house, making a real effort in school, and in practicing a musical instrument, sports, or any extracurricular activity. But avoid giving them more than is needed to match what their peers have available.

Where a serious interest is developing, do all you can to support practicing or learning that skill. For example, a ukulele or harmonica can be an initial means to show whether your child might have a talent for music. A simple camera or paint set can test artistic skills. It is not necessary to have the best quality instrument for an initial introduction. But expect to be asked for better and better equipment that you can hopefully acquire "used."

Lastly, get in touch with a successful person in the activity that interests your child. Arrange for them to get together in order to discuss the opportunities and challenges in that area. If possible, supply books about successful people in that field to enlarge their understanding.

FOR TEACHERS: All of your students are not going to become entrepreneurs, of course. But several will show they have the potential to not only excel, but be a leader in a specific area. These "stars" may be the ones who are easiest to teach, but don't let that mean you give them less attention. Your extra efforts with a star will have greater pay-offs.

Ask your budding entrepreneurs to help you prepare or clean the classroom, assist students having difficulties, or perhaps work on the displays for "Parents Night." Give them a chance to lead a project team.

Let parents know of the responsibility they have to keep their child challenged. Work with them to coordinate activities outside of the classroom.

FOR BUSINESS MANAGERS: It is satisfying to present opportunities for young people to become entrepreneurs in business. Publicize openings for students. Look for young people who ask you for a job, who are aggressive but polite, who smile but look you in the eye, and who are articulate but do not speak excessively. Let them know how they can make a better impression on their next interview.

Have work rules in writing. Make sure a new employee receives and understands these rules. Don't let them break a rule twice without a very good reason. You must realize that school and parental needs have first priority, but excessive excuses are a basis for termination.

You or an associate should mentor these high school interns to ensure they are developing good work habits. Try to stretch what they can do, even if it has some elements of risk. I am still grateful to the manager of the Weis Market who helped teach me the skill of selling.

If deserving, offer to write a letter of reference for these students. Explain to the student why you might not be able to recommend him/her to future employers. Hopefully, the student will do better, if given a second chance.

Chapter 2

Taking Risks Through College

FOR ASPIRING ENTREPRENEURS, college provides a plethora of opportunities:

1. To make some extra money, preferably in an area of educational interest.

2. To provide valuable contacts, both with professors and classmates, that will endure for the rest of your life.

3. To get valuable experience in a laboratory or business, even if it is a non-paying internship.

This experience may be coupled to one's "room and board" choice, such as becoming the house manager in a dormitory or fraternity. Sometimes it is working with a professor on a project beyond the requirements of the course, or choosing an extra tough course over an easy elective. It may be an extracurricular activity, such as singing in a chapel choir. There are all sorts of activities that are not all that time-consuming, as might be the case with a college sports team. It might be finding a part-time job at the local hospital. One of my friends spent his nights manning a hospital switchboard while doing his homework.

There is really no end to what entrepreneurs can do to expand their knowledge, give them new experiences, earn money, and enlarge their circle of friends and professional references. A huge benefit of such activities is the reference to them that can be added to your resume, or the stories that can be used in interviews when pursuing a summer or permanent job.

It is possible that, in high school, you were so busy with work, study, or extracurricular activities, thinking about leadership or taking risks simply was not possible. It is not too late. College is an opportunity for a fresh start on taking risks: on courses elected, girls dated, jobs pursued, research projects started, friends cultivated, fraternities chosen, summer jobs sought, and trips selected. This will be the most exciting time of your life.

Recognize the fact that on college graduation, finding a permanent job will be your most important challenge. Yes, grades will be important, but what you have accomplished in your college years, beyond the academic requirements, may very well determine if you or someone else gets that prize job. No interviewer will believe you studied and attended class 50 hours a week and did nothing else. How did you spend the rest of your time? What did you do to prepare yourself to be an exceptional employee, an entrepreneur, in whatever activities you become involved? Don't let your college years go to waste.

The next section is an accounting of my six years of higher education, in which I got a B.S., an M.S. and a Ph.D. in Chemical Engineering—in addition to having two excellent paid summer internships. Perhaps I was crazy to be in such a hurry. In retrospect, I feel it was not really necessary to finish that quickly nor would I recommend such an accelerated pace. But, it was during this time that I first started thinking about being a leader, not just another graduate coming out looking for a job. What I describe here will only give you some clues as to what is possible.

Obviously, your first priority has to be on your course work. That is the minimum requirement, and there will still be time for the "fun stuff" of college life, important as you mature into adulthood. But what will differentiate you from the rest of the graduates is what you do that is useful beyond the course work. With what exceptional or entrepreneurial activity did you become involved that will excite the job interviewer and result in your being invited for a visit and an internship, or even a permanent job?

So, it's June, 1945. The war in Europe is over and ex-GIs are coming home to resume their interrupted college studies. Penn State had gone to a three-semester system of annual classes. I'm barely 17 years old, but I can't wait to get my undergraduate degree as soon as possible.

In the previous chapter, I discussed risk-taking activities during high school. This would be the ideal, but is perhaps too much to expect for busy teenagers. However, by college, habits are becoming set. Students who just do what is required to pass their courses—we all have seen many of them—will tend to "work" the same way after college. So now it is becoming imperative that some of the time at college needs to be directed at more than just completing academic courses.

In some cases, a student is required to work full time for financial reasons, making it difficult to also achieve academic excellence. Hopefully, an outside job can present opportunities to do more than is expected. In the act of doing more, the job can give the student a chance to earn money for the limited time available for work. In addition, the work can allow him/her to test their "wings" at taking risks.

But for the student who does not need to work full-time, having some extracurricular activities beyond classes and studies can be very important to their health and mind, as well as the personal resumes they will use to find permanent employment after school.

This chapter is purely biographical. No one else will have the exact same opportunities or interest that I had. On many occasions, however, my aggressiveness created entrepreneurial opportunities that had significant impact during my post-graduate career. I had no idea of how valuable my risk-taking would be.

For parents, it is important to strategize with their child about how college will be financed. I was very fortunate: while my father and mother were not wealthy, they expected their three children would go to college. They were hoping we would be qualified for and excited about a state college or a modest private university.

Loans and scholarships for students were not too common in the 1940s, but today a large percent of good students can reasonably hope to at least partially reduce or defray their tuition costs.

Whatever the family situation may be, having an understanding with the student on what is expected is very important. Living costs at college can vary by as much as a factor of four, ranging from residing at a top-rated fraternity/sorority versus living as frugally as possible. In my situation, I had a savings account worth $1,000, or about $16,000 in today's dollars. My dad matched that and it was all I needed.

Admittedly, my tuition only cost $50 per year, my living costs were modest, and I worked 10 hours a week. Believe me, that still left plenty of time for studies and having a full college experience. Out of curiosity more than necessity, for my first two years, I kept a journal of every dollar I spent. My dad never asked to see it, but he knew I was not wasting money. It was an excellent learning experience for me.

EARNING SPENDING MONEY

Following my high school graduation on June 12, 1945, and the two-week chemistry briefing, I moved to Pennsylvania State College, as it was then called. I had previously arranged to share a double-occupancy room at only $3.50 a week in a private home that provided rooms for eight male students. In the next couple of days, I was courted by a fraternity, Pi Kappa Alpha, but noted that most of the members were ex-GI's—great guys but mature and with cars and money. I wasn't really compatible so found the type of cooperative that should be a required organization at every university. The Nittany Co-op, a block from my rooming house, rented two houses, the larger one having enough room to serve three meals a day to 70 people. Above the large first-floor lounge, kitchen, and dining hall (and in the adjoining home) were rooms for approximately 35 co-eds.

Being a co-op, everyone was required to contribute 3-4 hours of work each week. My first job was to wash dishes three nights a week; in time my assignments became less boring. In return, my meals, which were comparable to fraternity meals, cost only $1 per day. The 35 males who came in from neighboring rooming houses were also older than me, but had less money and fewer cars than the fraternity students. This was a wonderful experience. The co-ed feature helped me learn to really dance, play bridge, and have lots of fun with other "co-opers." We were all in a hurry to get through college and one big advantage was that, like a fraternity, we had a file of old tests from many of the courses. Best of all, we learned to work together as a team, sharing responsibility. We were family.

It also offered leadership opportunities through committees for each function. My favorite was chairing a subcommittee to buy a few new popular records each month. That function helped me sharpen my skills in handling my friends whose records were not chosen.

Yes, even joining a co-op for my college meals was a risk, but one I would rank near the top of those I took my freshman year.

From the first day of class, I found my high school experience had prepared me well for Penn State. With time on my hands, I found a part-time job helping a wonderful professor, Dr. Mary Willard, maintain the laboratory associated with her courses on chemical microscopy. When friends heard about this job, they wondered how I had gotten it. I had simply taken the risk of inquiring around the campus about jobs and then asking for it.

The students in this class learned to take photographs through special microscopes, which meant that a dark room was required. In the evenings once or twice a week, I would prepare fresh solutions for developing and printing photos. Dr. Willard said if I supplied my own photo paper, I was welcome to use the darkroom. In a way, that allowed me to check the quality of the solutions prepared.

Ha! While I had my own camera and took a few photographs, my primary developing and printing were done on photos of nudes supplied by some of my older friends. Imagine being paid by the hour and having this opportunity. But I can tell you that in all my time there, I never printed one good photograph.

In August, football practice began, and with returning ex-GIs, an excellent team was expected. Wanting to follow up on my secret desire to be a part-time sportscaster, I asked the press specialist for Penn State teams if I could work in the press box "spotting players." While he could not give me that job, which the gymnastic coach had held for years, I could have a job keeping statistics if I were willing to do that. Incredible! Now I had the best seat in the stadium doing what I most loved next to spotting players. In addition, I could participate in a buffet available to the press box reporters and staff. To this 17-year-old boy, who was maturing and adding 6 inches in height in one year, this was a dream job. No pay, but what wonderful benefits.

Each season, I got more responsibility in the press box, and, during my final autumn at PSU, I spotted players for the first Nittany Lion game that was ever televised. The gymnastic coach didn't know what he was missing. Another wonderful experience I received by taking the risk of asking and then accepting a lesser assignment.

One highlight during my first semester was a talk by Dean Frank Whitmore on how A-bombs work. This was only days after Hiroshima and made me even more excited about taking science courses. We were the best-informed students on campus. In no time, the semester was over and I was elected to a freshman honors society. My parents were delighted.

With a week between semesters and some holidays, the three-semester system worked. More GIs joined my chemical engineering class of about 50. I did take time to maintain my usual activities and even to sing in a student choir, but I kept in mind that doing well in class was my first priority.

DIVERSE EXPERIENCES

After my first two college years, I was elected to the engineering honors society, Tau Beta Pi, and worked my way up to become the treasurer and a member of the selection committee. This selection process was a learning experience, with many more students being nominated than could be accepted. As an independent student, I observed how fraternity members tried to promote their candidates. I tried not to let my own organizational biases influence me too much. That was not easy.

In two calendar years, by attending classes through the summers, I had gotten through 6 semesters of courses and completed my junior year. I was really looking forward to a summer job as a student chemical engineer.

Thanks to that wonderful Dean Whitmore, whom I had gotten to know, I received an offer for a summer job in the Engineering Department of Sun Oil Company. I was one of 12 chemists and chemical engineers chosen. We all were about to enter our senior years at colleges ranging from the Ivy League to the Big 10. I suspect that the positive recommendation I got from Dr. Whitmore was the reason I was selected. It was my reward for my taking the risk to introduce myself, and his getting to know me. You never know.

We worked in the Sun Oil refinery and laboratories located in Marcus Hook, not exactly the garden spot of Pennsylvania. Fortunately, Sun arranged for us to occupy wonderful student rooms at Swarthmore College in a gorgeous "mainline" town near Philadelphia. We were 20 minutes away from the laboratory and only worked from 8 to 5. This gave us lots of time for tennis, bridge, reading, and complaining about the mothers of Swarthmore who would not permit their tennis-playing daughters to date the "riff raff" staying over for the summer. Periodically, we would take the train to Philadelphia and one weekend we went to New York City. The only negative was that my work in the refinery, though interesting, had no relationship to research. Some of my buddies were chemists and had much more interesting assignments. That convinced me that for an engineer to do research, it helped to have a graduate degree.

So, in the winter of my senior year, I applied to the top chemical engineering graduate schools in the country. The University of Illinois offered me a teaching fellowship that would cover all my tuition and pay me $100 per month. That made the decision fairly easy. I was fortunate to have had a chemical engineering professor at Penn State, Dr. Floyd Carnahan, who took a special interest in me and must have written an excellent letter of reference. Again, I benefited from making friends with superiors who could be so helpful in advancing my career.

ON TO GRADUATE SCHOOL

My job as a teaching assistant at the University of Illinois was to grade papers and conduct quiz sessions twice a week with 25 junior chemical engineering students. They also attended a weekly lecture on heat transfer by one of the professors. Thanks to that job, I really learned heat transfer more thoroughly than I had ever learned it when I originally took the course. I also monitored a four-hour weekly laboratory session that was really enjoyable and made me more conscious of laboratory safety issues than I had realized as a student.

My course work required more effort than college, but was manageable and I appreciated the importance of what I was learning more than ever. When Dr. Harry Drickamer, teaching a course in advanced separations, taught us to use a McCabe-Thiele diagram for determining the performance of a distillation column in the separation of two components, he stated that as far as he knew, no one had learned how to use that diagram if there were three components. He clearly stated that if someone learned to do that, it would be worth a technical article in a chemical engineering journal.

Alone among the students, I took the risk of trying to prove it possible. I worked that evening until 3 a.m. and proved it could be done. When I showed him my solution, he said "that's great," but welshed on the paper. In spite of that, I chose him and he agreed to be the director for my master's thesis. During the spring and summer of that first year, I completed the thesis, fulfilling the requirements of the Masters degree.

That summer, Dr. Drickamer redeemed himself by recommending me for a General Electric research scholarship. Like the teaching assistantship, it paid all my college costs and gave me $100 a month to cover living expenses. It allowed me to start working on my Ph.D. thesis at the start of my second year in graduate school with no teaching responsibility. As expected, I signed up to be among Dr. Drickamer's thesis students. By now he was "Doc" to me, and when he had a student who needed some help in monitoring experiments overnight, I agreed—a small risk of my time. To be alone in the lab all night was not my idea of a fun event, but I enjoyed reading and would catch up on my sleep later. Also, in a year or two, I might need the same help. One of these experiments that required multiple nights of my time had to do with "thermal diffusion"—a practically unknown method for separating gases. In fact, it had been the initial way that uranium had been enriched into the U-235 isotope. But our experiments were only dealing with separating different carbon isotopes using carbon dioxide gas. Radioactive Carbon 13 served as the trace element.

Doc Drickamer also had an idea about how one could calculate the separation factor for gaseous isotopes near their critical point. Ed Geller, the student doing the thermal-diffusion experiments, was getting the data that might prove Doc's theory, but he was not doing the theoretical work. Unfortunately, the computational requirements on hand calculators in 1950 meant that a hundred hours of computations were needed, which neither Doc nor Ed wanted to do. I volunteered and, after six months, two papers were written and published in the prestigious *Journal of Chemical Physics*. Doc included my name as an author on these two papers. Little did I know how important that was going to be to my later career.

In my fourth semester at Illinois, for the first time, there was the opportunity to take a non-requisite course. Doc said that there was a young math professor, named Harry Laz, who was teaching a new course on "special functions." While my buddies were selecting easy courses, like English lit or economics, I took the risk and registered for this course, being the first engineer to ever sign up for it. It was the toughest course I ever took. To my delight, however, I found it exhilarating to learn about Laplace transforms and Laguerre polynomials, with no idea of how such advanced mathematics would ever be used by a chemical engineer.

Even though Doc did not take the course, he loved hearing about what I was learning. And, four years later, I would use the math on a work project that no other associate was prepared to tackle.

By the end of the second year, I had completed my coursework, and only needed to pass the qualifying exam that would let me work full-time on my research. For several days, the five chemical engineering students on the same schedule as me all sat together studying, hoping we would all pass, and absolutely not caring in what order our grades were. Failures would have set our schedule back by at least six months. When we learned later that we had all passed, we had the best celebration since I graduated from Penn State.

ACCELERATED DOCTORAL TRACK

With that behind me, and a research scholarship paying my tuition plus $100 per month, I was set for 100% concentration on my research leading to a Ph.D. thesis and degree.

Doc said if I would work 72 hours a week on my thesis project, I might finish in a year. Without hesitation, I agreed, and often checked my schedule to keep my end of the bargain. Then the graduate fraternity where I lived asked if I would be the "house manager" for a year. The duties primarily consisted of paying all the bills, collecting the monthly rent from each fraternity member, keeping the books, giving a monthly report to the members, and keeping the cook happy. This turned out to be an excellent learning experience. Double-entry bookkeeping was an education in itself and to get free room-and-board for this was a great deal. I actually saved money while going to school and being responsible for keeping both the hired cook and my fraternity brothers happy. It was also a great learning experience.

Much of my research time involved designing and building the equipment required to measure the self-diffusion rate of carbon dioxide gas around its critical point. This was part of Doc Drickamer's effort to explore the behavior of dense gases, hopefully leading to an understanding of transport properties of materials from the ideal gas state to dense liquids. My measurements would be the first effort to analytically measure "self-diffusion" in dense gas at high pressure and around a "critical point."

My diffusion cell needed to be made out of steel, which required me to learn how to operate a lathe and milling machine. Since this diffusion cell was required to contain radioactive carbon dioxide at high pressure, its design and construction was quite a test for a chemical engineer. But that is part of what a Ph.D. thesis is to accomplish (*i.e.*, teach students how to become expert in the physical skills required in a laboratory in order to teach oneself other new skills needed in the future).

While no additional classes were required of me, I could audit a course if I had an interest. Fortunately, a professor had created a new course in radioactivity and I gladly took the risk of enrolling, which turned out to be helpful for my project.

I was also learning about newly acquired photo-multipliers, fluorescent crystals, pre-amps, amplifiers, and scalers—all of which had to work simultaneously to perform the diffusion measurements. The design, construction, and assembly of this system took eight months. By the early spring of my third year at Illinois, I was able to make only one or two measurements per day if I kept the usual hours of many graduate students (*i.e.*, eight hours per day). I found it beneficial to keep running additional experiments once the system was working and decided that in a week of continuous operation, I could probably get 60 different measurements made, each at a different carbon dioxide temperature and pressure. One week in April, with all the electronics working, I began running experiments at 8 a.m. on Monday and kept going non-stop until Saturday noon. I had naps at the end of each test, when recording of scaler data only needed to be made every 15 minutes. (Today, students would have automatic recorders, but not in 1951). No problem. I had a cot by the scaler and a laboratory alarm would awaken me every 15 minutes for the last hour of every four-hour experiment. I would not want my mother to have seen the junk food I was imbibing, but during that week I recorded 50% of the data required for my thesis. Drickamer was impressed. He was in as much of a hurry for the data as I was and by staying in the lab all week, I did not need to train a volunteer helper. (By the way, after a nap on Saturday afternoon, I picked up my date and went to a university ball that night.)

For another month, there were sporadic experiments to run, but I knew I was on the home stretch and all I had left was the actual writing of the thesis. On August 15, the final oral examination would determine if I was to receive my Ph.D.

An interesting anecdote from the oral examination which covered my thesis, plus anything else I was supposed to have learned from my courses, was a question asked me by Dr. Harry Laz, the special functions mathematics professor. Fortunately I could answer it, and Dr. Drickamer said of all the oral exams he had attended in seven years at Illinois, this was the first time one of his students was asked a question that he himself could not answer.

GETTING TO KNOW GE

During the spring of this final year, I did take time to make job-seeking visits to Monsanto, DuPont, Esso, and General Electric. It was an easy decision to join the Knolls Atomic Power Laboratory, managed by General Electric, in Schenectady, N.Y. This laboratory was developing a nuclear reactor for Admiral Rickover's submarines, and that sounded like an endeavor that would help the country and give me an introduction into the emerging nuclear power industry. There is no doubt that this GE research fellowship gave me a warm feeling toward the company and I have never regretted my decision.

Compared to my graduate friends at Illinois, who took anywhere from three-and-one-half to five years to obtain their Ph.D.s, I felt that 72 hours of work each week had not hurt me in any way and I set a record of three years—the shortest time in which anyone at Illinois in chemical engineering has earned a Ph.D. In addition, my entrepreneurial efforts to help other students run their experiments and to perform the calculations I did for Dr. Drickamer resulted in two published papers beyond my own thesis publication. And serving as house manager for the fraternity probably did not hurt either.

I was very pleased with the variety of accomplishments and experiences I could include on my resume during my subsequent job search.

CONCLUSIONS

As I look back on college, these are actions that prepared me for an exciting career and also gave me an outstanding resume for my future job pursuit.

TO STUDENTS: An entrepreneur likes setting records, breaking new ground, doing challenging things no one else volunteers to do.

An entrepreneur looks for learning experiences, like being a sorority or fraternity president, or working nights at an ice cream parlor. And, as a bonus, it may bring in extra cash.

An entrepreneur helps his friends succeed in school, as long as it's ethical. Sharing in studies is perfectly alright; doing someone else's work is not.

An entrepreneur positively responds to a mentor who pushes or stimulates him. He may well find that extra challenges are more valuable than might be obvious at the time. When a student finds such a mentor, he values the relationship and will go out of his way to complete projects that help the mentor become more successful.

An entrepreneur finds unusual opportunities to enjoy college and get valuable experiences he can talk about. For example, don't just go to sports events, but find a way to get involved: spot players from the press box, or become the student manager for a sports team, a dancer, band member, etc. Don't just go to weekly chapel on Sundays, but be in the choir, an usher, or otherwise participate in the service. Don't just join an organization, but become a leader, committee chairperson, etc.

The value of a doctoral degree is very dependent on the professor with whom the student arranges to work. It is perhaps as important as the school, and choosing an entrepreneurial professor is strongly advised. Don't be in a rush to choose: learn from other students how each professor interacts with his students. Does he enjoy discussions with them? Does he avoid spending a lot of time away from campus on consulting assignments? Do his students get papers published in reputable journals? Does he have a significant reputation in his specialty area? I am grateful that Doc Drickamer met all these criteria.

TAKING RISKS WITHOUT SUCCESS

If you get the feeling that every risk I took worked out, nothing could be further from the truth. The first month that I was at Penn State, I flunked the audition to become a clarinetist in the college's formal "Blue Band." They let me play in the band at football games, but then I found out that I had a job working in the press box and never played my clarinet again.

I signed on to be a reporter for *The Penn State Engineer*, a monthly magazine. Halfway through my first assignment, I realized this position was not for me.

At the co-op, by my senior year, I had become a pretty good ping-pong player. In the Spring Championship series, I got to the championship round but lost. Sad to say, I went through college without receiving one sports award.

Most importantly, I took the risk of really liking two co-eds, one at a time. They both warned me that their old boyfriends were in military service and that I would be dumped when they returned. Sure enough, I never managed another date with either girl.

In college, these things are all important, but not as important as the class work. So I guess you could say I had my priorities right. At least I was always willing to take another risk.

TO DEANS AND PROFESSORS: You are so important to encouraging leadership among your students. They will make a difference in the country's future and may even benefit your own careers. Every day, you will have opportunities to make a difference to students. Yes, it may involve taking risk. But if you are not, you are not fulfilling your responsibilities.

Some suggestions, based on my experiences:

- Keep your lectures timely; relate to world events. When Dean Whitmore, in August, 1945, told us freshman how the A-bomb worked and how chemists helped in its development, our interest in choosing a science career increased ten-fold.

- Use every opportunity to include ethical principles in your lessons.

- Use current news to make a point.

- Challenge your brightest students who can keep up with the normal class assignments in a fraction of the normal time with extra opportunities. These are not additional assignments, but a chance to really understand the subject and its applications.

- Pose extensions of the theories being presented (*e.g.*, what are the results of multiple component separations in unusual environments?).

- Encourage students to "do more than is required."

- Take the risk of hiring a student or two, thus helping them financially, then closely mentor their performance. Since they may ask you for a letter of reference, let them know if their efforts haven't yet justified one.

- Network yourself to establish relationships with professors in your discipline at other institutions. These connections can be useful in helping your senior students find the best graduate opportunities.

- Do the unexpected once in awhile. I remember that my college German professor one morning threw the entire class out the door in the middle of the period. We weren't worth her efforts, she said. Her taking the risk of such outrageous behavior made us study harder.

- Be willing to take risks with your teaching or grading methods with the aim of improving the learning process. How can you help the school or department head do better? Are you networking with other professors, exchanging good ideas, looking for synergies between courses? Are you proposing new courses you might co-teach?

- Make every effort to recruit students to take your courses, or high school students to sign up at your college and your department. Are you making presentations to young people, interesting them about your area of expertise? It would be easy today for me to make chemical engineering exciting to young people, and even to high school English teachers (unlike when I was a high school senior writing that contest essay).

Risk is not a popular trait in academic circles. Thankfully, I had the good fortune to have had several professors who took risks with me and I did not want to fail them.

Chapter 3

Taking Risks as an Individual Contributor

FOLLOWING SIX FULL-TIME YEARS OF COLLEGE, I couldn't wait to start my professional career. All I had in mind was to become the best chemical engineer possible. I hoped at some point to manage a few younger engineers and technicians to help make progress faster, but I was really looking forward to getting my hands "dirty," as we referred to working in a lab. I wanted an assignment with some importance, and the Knolls Atomic Power Laboratory (KAPL) would give me that opportunity.

LIFE AT THE BENCH

The group I joined consisted of seven chemical engineers, plus several technicians. The manager had a Masters degree and 20 years experience in a chemical company before he joined KAPL. I was the only Ph.D. in this group, though the manager in a second chemical engineering unit also had a doctorate. Gloria Foy, our unit secretary, helped keep everything running smoothly.

To my surprise, my new manager offered me a couple of weeks to look around, get familiar, and then make a proposal for a project that would be helpful to KAPL's mission. It did not work. I was overwhelmed with all I was learning and the idea I proposed and he accepted was, in retrospect, doubtful in two ways: could it work and, even if it did, would it really be important to KAPL's mission?

Fortunately, the Chemistry Laboratory manager bailed me out with the challenge to develop a process for coating a uranium fuel element with vapor-deposited zirconium. I read and talked to older researchers who suggested I design a new vacuum system, which might take a month to obtain from the glass shop. I was too impatient for that, so I scrounged equipment not being used and in two weeks I was ready for a test.

The first experiment showed I could deposit zirconium on a uranium sample much more easily than had been expected. I was off to a terrific start. Getting results so quickly with available equipment turned out to be a risk worth taking.

Had I spent a month reading and planning, as was expected, I could not have been further ahead. My entrepreneurial nature was demonstrated, once I was told what to work on. No one ever knew how relieved I was to be given my first project.

A month after coming to KAPL, another opportunity was presented to all the new engineers hired in the summer of 1951. The laboratory director offered a course on nuclear reactor design to new employees that would be taught over the next 9 months, with the instructional period being every other Friday from 8 to 5. The offer included a warning notice that homework was expected to take 10 hours per week outside of working hours. Homework would be turned in at each class, and engineers who did not keep up would be dismissed. My best buddy and I laughed: it would never take 10 hours per week for the homework. Expecting maybe a few hours, we both signed up for the course. Most new engineers were turned off by the warning and missed the opportunity to take the course.

From the very first class, we realized the instructor was not kidding. It took us 20 hours per class to complete the assignments. But what we were learning was so interesting and valuable to understanding this nuclear industry that we accepted the burden and were good students.

Equally valuable was not becoming accustomed to all the free time we would have had if we only worked 40 hours a week. By the end of the course, my work was sufficiently developed that I needed at least 50 hours a week for it. This was now where I placed all my efforts, not having gotten accustomed to 40 hours as did too many new employees who did not take the course.

Offering that course and making it tough was smart company management. My saying "yes" was an entrepreneurial decision. Some other friends who had just joined the company choose to skip this challenge. Sure, I envied them all their free time for bowling, golf, heavy dating, and taking weekend trips. However, as a single fellow, even with working and studying 50 hours a week, I had enough time to socialize, meet the wonderful co-ed I would marry, take a hiking trip to Mount Washington, and visit New York City occasionally.

But I had to manage my time. KAPL management saw who was willing to do more than was required right from the start.

The next year, the company offered a statistics course that only required a few hours to complete the homework each week. Again, I signed up for that course and at the end of the year, they asked if I would teach the course in the future. I was also invited by management to give presentations to local service organizations, such as the Rotary Club, on the popular topic of "nuclear energy." Eventually, I became involved with the employee social organization, becoming co-chair of a five-year KAPL birthday celebration that was talked about for weeks after the event. (Back in 1953, a secretarial "Charleston" dance line was considered very exciting.) By taking risks beyond the normal job requirements, I was becoming known to top management.

Even while working on my nuclear fuel coating project, I now, unlike two years earlier, came up with ideas for new projects that would enhance our chemical engineering unit and would fit into the KAPL budget. Even though these projects were assigned to other engineers in the unit, management knew where the ideas came from and a few of them were even patented.

ANOTHER OPPORTUNITY

After about two years on this assignment, enough progress had been made to transfer development to a pilot operation that would scale up my research system to deposit a zirconium coating on a full-sized Hanford fuel element. I was a consultant to this scale-up, and began working on a new research project to separate plutonium isotopes. A month or so into the project, the head of the laboratory called me into his office and informed me that we had been assigned the task of designing a thermal diffusion plant to be built at the Savannah River nuclear plant for the separation of hydrogen isotopes. This operation, in Georgia, would be managed by DuPont; the output of the plant would be tritium, the heaviest isotope of hydrogen and the key ingredient of H-bombs. He further stated that Oak Ridge National Laboratory had measured the separation factor between the six different molecules possible from the three isotopes of hydrogen and there wasn't enough tritium in the world to build a pilot plant. He asked me to head this project and to simulate on a computer the thermal diffusion columns that would make up this cascade. Time had been arranged on the second UNIVAC computer in the world, located in New York City, and I would be assigned a young software specialist who would be able to actually write the code for the computation. We would need additional security clearance to work on this project.

To say I was surprised is an understatement. I responded, "Why am I being picked to head this project?" His answer was that KAPL had looked through its database on all its 1,000 engineers and my resume was the only one that mentioned thermal diffusion. I thought back to the two papers I had co-authored with Professor Drickamer and the nighttime monitoring of a thermal diffusion column for a fellow graduate student. Who would ever have thought that this plum assignment would result from that extra work I had done in graduate school. Unfortunately, this was a super-secret project, which prevented me from telling Professor Drickamer what was happening, but I looked forward to the day when I could share the story with him.

For the next year, I worked on this project while continuing part-time on my experimental program. When the final report on the plant simulation was turned over to Savannah River, my special clearance was terminated, and for years, I was not sure what had happened to the design. Eventually, I did hear that the plant was built using the software program I created. It worked and I was finally able to tell Doc Drickamer about this project.

My experience over these five years had been fulfilling and educational. I was well rewarded, but I worried that KAPL was beginning to work more on incremental improvements on their nuclear engines and less on research projects where I had become one of their most entrepreneurial researchers. Fortunately, half a mile away was the General Electric Research Laboratory, renowned for its research breakthroughs to support GE businesses.

My reputation had reached them and, when I was offered a promotion in grade and pay to go there, I decided to move. It was difficult because I loved what I had accomplished at KAPL and the confidence it had given me to risk even bolder projects in a research laboratory.

A PROFESSIONAL UPGRADE

So, in December 1956, I moved to the GE Research Lab's Chemical Process Unit. My initial assignment was to work with another chemical engineer, who was making progress on a project for the lighting business, but at a slower rate than expected.

I did not mind getting started this way and, before long, I had my own project to help the lighting business make tungsten wire for lamp filaments at its Cleveland plant. My job was to analyze a new process that they could license to make elemental tungsten and, especially, to price what this process might cost. I asked what the present process cost, but they either considered that too proprietary or did not want me to know, perhaps fearing that the information might influence my costing of the new process.

Taking what I could learn about the existing process and using chemical engineering metrics, I got my own estimate of what the current process was costing. When they saw the results, they acknowledged they were foolish to have kept it so secret. I believe they even learned some things to make the existing process less expensive. But now they were more excited in how I would price their new process. As it turned out, my recommendation was that they not change processes. It was unusual for a Research Lab scientist to suggest that a changeover not be made to a new process. But sometimes saying "don't change" can win an award.

My next project was also unusual. It required monitoring a high-temperature reaction for more than 24 hours at a time. While I could have requested two technicians to take the 4–12 evening shift and the 12–8 morning shift, I asked my technician to work from 8 am–6 pm and I would come in overnight. It reminded me of graduate school and my overnight monitoring for my thesis project. It demonstrated to Laboratory management that I was willing to work odd hours if it reduced the cost and the time required to complete the project.

GAS PERMEABLE MEMBRANES

About the time I was completing my report and filing a patent application on the previous project, I was asked by my boss to take a look at a proposal for a new gas separating membrane. It was proposed by the associate laboratory director, who loved to invent new processes but counted on others to put them into practice. This had no connection to thermal diffusion; it involved taking plastic films and bombarding them with different types of radiation, with the expectation that the radiation "track" through the film would permeate different gases at different rates. I worked on this diligently, including consulting with many scientists in the Laboratory. I finally had to tell the associate director that it wouldn't work. While that was disappointing to both of us, it is interesting to note what came out of those experiments.

In reading about membranes for gas separation, my research disclosed that GE's silicone business already made a polymer that was 20 times as permeable as normal plastics, and that it had different permeability rates for different gases. The problem was that, while most polymers could be formed into thin, hole-free films, silicone rubber had been impossible to make hole-free in a 1-mil thick film. This was a result of its weak rubbery nature and the presence of gel particles, which always seemed to be present in silicone rubber.

After trying for a month to make hole-free membranes, my technician and I discovered that if we took two 1-mil thick films of silicone rubber and pressed and bonded them together, using atmospheric pressure on an evacuated platform, we could make 2-mil thick membranes that were essentially hole-free. Yes, it was possible that microscopic holes in both membranes could coincide, but we invented a leak-check method that would identify these very rare holes and they could be patched with silicone RTV. Then we learned that we could stretch the 2-mil film in both directions until it was only 1-mil thick. Lo and behold, we had the world's most permeable hole-free membrane.

Of interest, carbon dioxide would permeate this film five times as fast as oxygen; oxygen would permeate twice as fast as nitrogen. It turns out that these rates are not totally dissimilar from the permeation rate of the tissue in a human lung. Obviously, this might be an approach to making an artificial lung. It also is not dissimilar from the membrane in the gill of a fish, which led to the idea of making an artificial gill. I discovered that if a mouse were placed in a one cubic foot box with the sides covered with a supported silicone film, and the box then put under circulating aerated water, the silicone membrane would keep liquid water out of the box while permitting two different permeation effects: oxygen would permeate from the water into the cage; and carbon dioxide would permeate out of the cage and into the water. Interestingly, the oxygen pressure in the cage leveled out at 16% of normal atmosphere, comparable to living at an altitude of 12,000 feet. The carbon dioxide level had increased to 1 percent, which was less than the Navy maintained in its submarines at that time.

BRIEF STARDOM

The company decided this was worth a press release, and a 1-foot cubic cage was built with its front and backsides constructed of transparent polycarbonate sheet. The other four sides had a mesh screen covered with a porous paper on which the silicone membrane was stretched. The cage contained the food supply for a hamster and was immersed in a water tank, with the fresh water being circulated around the four membrane sides of the cage. In the press release, I was shown looking through the clear faces of the cage and the water tank, observing the hamster happily alive underwater, surrounded by an artificial gill.

This caught the attention of the press far beyond our expectations, and made the cover of *Life* magazine in 1963. I was interviewed on Walter Cronkite's TV news show and on a half-hour science program. Schools loved this project since students saw for themselves how a human lung and a fish gill work for the first time. The U.S. Navy even explored the possibility of utilizing this gill in their operations and concluded that the energy to move the gill through the water would limit its applications. But the most useful defense application had to do with the possibility of extracting carbon dioxide from the exhaled air of a fighter pilot. Unfortunately, the separation factor between carbon dioxide and oxygen was 5.5, too low to be practical. But now I knew what my target was: to find a way to increase that separation factor. Frustrated by the difficulty of making membranes of new polymeric compositions, I conceived of a test cell that could measure the permeation through a liquid film. At least that would be easier than making plastic films of new compositions, and sufficient for conducting experiments.

My first film was water and the CO_2/O_2 separation factor was 5.5—identical to silicone rubber. If I increased the alkalinity of the water, the separation factor went up quickly; we eventually found an organic base that had a separation factor of 1,000 to 1. This resulted in a paper that I was invited to present at a NATO conference in Ravello, Italy, a resort that Jackie Kennedy had made famous. To be able to introduce a concept of immobilized liquid membranes to 50 world scientists, all of whom were interested in membranes, was a thrill that still excites me. Today, hundreds of scientists are involved with this type of membrane that I introduced at that conference.

The conference, funded by NATO, was attended by invitees from 20 countries, including, for the first time, two scientists from the USSR. The conference itself took place at the Villa Cimbrone, a resort-hotel that hosted many distinguished musicians, writers, and celebrities.

Except for the conference chairman, the rest of the attendees, all of whom were given the opportunity to deliver a scientific paper, stayed at a more reasonably priced resort hotel within walking distance from the conference center. For our meals, we sat together at nine tables under a grape arbor. The food was unbelievably good, perhaps helped by the presence of two pitchers containing white and red wines on each table. All the speakers spoke some English and we had lots in common. I am sure that it was the most enjoyable five days of work I ever spent.

GOING NUCLEAR

About this time, the head of the Research Lab's Chemistry Department, Dr. Arthur Bueche, asked if I would serve on a committee being formed to explore auxiliary businesses for GE's nuclear business headquartered in Palo Alto, Calif. The strategic planning team would be chaired by the vice president of planning for the nuclear business, and consist of two experienced engineers from the Hanford Atomic Products Lab in Richland, Wash., a nuclear business engineer, and myself. The VP had actually been Director of the Knoll Atomic Power Laboratory shortly before I left there for the Research Laboratory. His knowledge about my experience at KAPL must have convinced him that I would be a worthy representative of the Research Laboratory. Once again, what happened years before provided a new, exciting opportunity.

I told Dr. Bueche that I would be delighted to take this expected three-month assignment, though Anne and I had a two-year old son and two-week old son at home. I proposed that if the company would pay for the family to travel to California and rent a motel-apartment for three months, it would probably be less expensive than sending me alone, expecting to have periodic trips back to Schenectady during this period. This was agreed to and I flew to San Francisco for the first meeting of the team. In no time, I found a perfect apartment for my family and, with my wife's parents helping with a commercial airline transfer at LaGuardia airport, Anne and our two sons had an uneventful trip to San Francisco. For the next 10 weeks, we had a wonderful time with gorgeous weather and only 10 minutes of rain during the entire time. The team did not get together on weekends and Anne found a competent babysitter. This allowed us to tour San Francisco and the countryside, as well as spend time with friends from KAPL who had transferred to the growing GE Nuclear business.

While the two Hanford engineers concentrated their efforts on whether GE should build a nuclear fuel element processing facility, I concentrated my efforts on whether the company should get into the uranium enrichment business and whether GE should build a plant to convert enriched uranium into uranium oxide powder that was used in the fuel elements of GE boiling water reactors. I guess my score here was 50%, since the company built the conversion plant but not the uranium enrichment plant. The negative decision regarding the fuel processing facility was based more on government regulations than economics.

The risk of boldly requesting that the family be moved to California worked out well for everyone. My wife and I enjoyed the weeks we had in sunny California and, more importantly, I solved a problem for my boss, Art Bueche.

Returning to Schenectady, I was asked to be on a recruiting team to the University of Illinois, specializing on chemical engineering graduates. Over a few visits, I saw four graduates join General Electric, one to work with me on immobilized liquid membranes and to take the process even further than I had.

But the most unusual hire was Jack Welch, who was finishing his Ph.D. thesis at Urbana-Champaign. Unlike all the other graduate students, he emphasized that his goal was to go with a business rather than work in a corporate research laboratory. Fortunately, I knew the plastic business was looking for a chemical engineer to be in charge of a new pilot plant. The job was expected to be filled by a B.S. or M.S. candidate, but when I told the head of the project about Jack, he hired him to manage the pilot plant. And so began Jack's fabulous career with GE. Little did I suspect the impact this placement would have on my own career.

After 10 years with the company, but still an individual contributor, I was asked by the Director of the Chemistry Department, Art Bueche, if I would consider a possible job at the Hanford nuclear operation in Hanford, Washington. The opening was for a director of an R & D section that was composed of approximately 30 scientists working on issues bearing on the nuclear reactors at the Hanford site. Not having been a manager before, I was amazed that Art recommended me and that they would not have a better candidate in the organization. It turned out that his support, plus my contributions to the nuclear studies in California a few years earlier, as well as my work on vapor-coating Hanford fuel elements, had received favorable attention from managers at the site. They did not want to waste their time and money for a visit if I were not willing to accept a good offer and move to Hanford. Art reinforced the importance of my being willing to at least consider the move, complaining about the difficulty of finding Laboratory candidates willing to consider excellent openings in various GE businesses.

After discussing the opportunity with my wife, we agreed it was worth my visiting, and I had an excellent meeting over two full days with several department managers in the Hanford operations. Upon my return, I waited and waited for a decision, and then was told that they had found a manager at KAPL whose section was being dissolved and he was being transferred to Hanford. Fortunately, I had not counted too highly on this opportunity, or spoken about it to many people. One close friend, a semi-retired department manager at the Laboratory, told me I was crazy to consider that move. To me, it was just part of my entrepreneurial nature and a risk worth taking. While I did not get the job, it was a win because I was willing to be considered and made a good impression with management. Of course, it also stirred my hopes of becoming a manager.

"OUTSIDE THE BOX" THINKING

Back at the R & D Center, I was invited to join an evening class composed of senior scientists and first-level managers aimed at improving our business knowledge by creating a business plan for a possible new product in General Electric. Split into teams, I was pleased we had a good cross-section: a chemist, a physicist, the machine shop manager, and myself. After a few classes, we chose to develop a product that the GE Radio Receiver business might find appealing. In addition to radios, they sold a variety of switches, double plugs, light sockets, and such. Our idea was to produce a remote switch, one part being a hand switch on a cord that could be plugged into any outlet in the house. The other part, which was also plugged into any outlet in the house, had a relay that could turn the electric current on and off to whatever was plugged into this second box. When a switch on the first box was turned on, it sent a weak low-frequency RF signal through the house wiring. That signal could be sensed by the circuit in the second box and it would turn the relay on, powering whatever was connected to that box. For example, one could use this device to turn on an electric blanket upstairs from a switch located in the living room. Outdoor Christmas lights could be turned on and off from the kitchen. We came up with more than a 100 applications.

Each team self-organized with R & D, marketing, and production managers. Perhaps since this idea was my proposal, I was selected to be the general manager. But we really worked as a team, not with three different silos. We chose "Electro-Butler" for the product name and built a nice prototype. When it worked to our satisfaction, we made three more so that each of us could take one home. We estimated the manufacturing cost, and were convinced it could sell for $15. We won the award for the best product, as determined by a jury of our peers.

Then we traveled to the Radio Receiver Department in Utica, N.Y., and made a presentation to the department manager and his staff. They were impressed, gave us a nice letter of appreciation, but decided not to add this to their product line.

We finally realized that it was probably too risky a product for General Electric. There is always a danger of remotely turning on power when you are not absolutely sure what may be attached to the outlet. In some cases, the RF signal could be transmitted to a second home.

Several years later, we saw our product marketed by a couple of small companies who did not have such deep pockets as GE. It was an interesting project and I loved being general manager.

A TASTE OF MANAGEMENT

My immediate boss was a good manager and treated me very well. He used me as his technical consultant on many occasions and appreciated my well-written, concise analyses that he could use with confidence. Then, in 1961, he was selected to attend the Business Management Course for three months at GE's Crotonville (N.Y.) Institute and I was asked to fill in for him. This not only involved managing the chemical engineering unit but also being a program manager for a cross-function team challenged with producing a thermoplastic tape to go into a combination tape recorder and projector that the physics lab was proposing to replace movie film.

During those 13 weeks, I had a suspicious feeling that one of the senior scientists on the tape project was advancing a theory on plastic flow that didn't meet my "common sense test." People feared to challenge him because he was so erudite in explaining his theory. Unfortunately, my suspicions and questioning proved to be correct, and in two months he had transferred out of the company, his theory having come apart.

The head of the Chemistry Department, Dr. Art Bueche, was pleased that I had been willing to challenge this senior scientist. He complimented me on my three-month temporary stewardship of the chemical engineering unit, but cautioned me to get back to my regular work and "be patient."

Between the regular research work and the unusual extra assignments that I was given, I was having a wonderful career. However, chemical engineers usually are expected to get involved in many different technologies, and it is unusual for one to become a world-class expert in one field. At a university, I might have accomplished that with my work on liquid membranes, but since that was unlikely to be possible here, the thought of becoming a manager based on my 13-week "acting" assignment became intense.

Out of the blue, a surprising announcement came concerning our manager, Norm Kirk, the head of the chemical engineering section. He had accepted a promotion in the GE Plastics business and within an hour I was at Art Bueche's door to let him know that I was interested in Norm's position.

A week later, as Norm was packing to leave, Art told me I had the job. It included a two level jump in pay, an annual bonus, and a stock option opportunity. In discussions, Art liked my performance when I filled in for Norm Kirk, he liked the letters I wrote for him for various company reviews, and was especially pleased that I was willing to move. He appreciated my willingness to take the risk of moving to Hanford if that would help the company. He said he would come to our building at 8 a.m. the following morning to make the announcement and that I was to "keep mum until then."

My wife was not surprised when I asked her over dinner, "Guess what happened today?"

LESSONS LEARNED

1. On accepting a new job, ask for assignments until you have had the time to learn as much as you can about the industry and your own company's activities. You'll have an opportunity, in proper time, to propose your own project.

2. Attack the first assignment with vigor, soliciting advice, probing, planning, and keeping your boss advised. Show your energy, passion, and commitment by doing more than expected. Help your co-workers where and when your efforts and ideas might be useful, but only to the extent your help is wanted. Take classes, teach courses, but restrict your efforts to areas that have potential relevance to your job.

3. Look for opportunities to give talks, or write reports on your work, as you get more acquainted with your business.

4. Propose new projects, new products, and more efficient ways to operate. Think "outside the box." Ask your peers how your knowledge and experience could be of benefit to them.

5. Help your boss look "good." The more he succeeds, the faster he will be promoted, which will promote your own career as well.

6. Be willing to move, if that is what the company asks of you. Don't accept ridiculous assignments, but accept the risk of a proposed assignment where you feel confident you will succeed.

7. Be involved in the social organization, but never to the detriment of your job.

8. Establish a reputation as an individual contributor before even considering becoming a manager.

TO FIRST-LEVEL MANAGERS: Your responsibilities extend beyond just supervising the work of individuals on your team. You are also responsible for their continuing education and advancement. Look for leaders and give them more than the usual responsibilities. Expose them to advanced-education opportunities and encourage them to network beyond your own group. Be willing to take a risk in giving them challenging assignments, but realize that not all ideas succeed.

Yes, you need to devote sufficient time to working with your problem employees, but the bigger payoffs may come from the attention you give to your "stars." How you develop new employees will be noticed by your supervisors.

You also have the responsibility of demonstrating the importance of your group to the rest of the organization. Kindle enthusiasm in your group to help you bring into motion proposed projects for the company.

Network with your peers, especially when their own teams are depending on advances that are the responsibility of your group members. Don't assume that your team is always on schedule.

Remember that some leaders are better off becoming experts in their fields. Help your employees to plan their career advancements, whether to management positions or technical specialist. Don't hesitate to recommend your promising people for promotion, even though it may detract from the abilities of your own team. Promotions make your group a better place for hiring the best candidates.

Chapter 4

Taking Risks as a First-time Manager

ONE MINUTE I was one of six scientists and five technicians left in the Chemical Engineering unit following the departure of our leader. Art Bueche, Chemistry Department Manager, had arrived at our Chemical Engineering building and the team was assembled. The next minute, I was appointed manager of this unit and, with a few kind words, Art was off to his office at the main building.

I had been working among these five scientists for the last six years, so this wasn't new territory. I was vaguely familiar with each person's program, and after a few words asking for their support, I set up individual interviews with each of them. This was aimed at refreshing my memory as to their plans and ties to various businesses in the company. By the next day, I was aware of only two problem areas.

One scientist was about to submit a paper for publication, which the departed manager had asked me to review. I was concerned that there was an erroneous assumption in the paper, which he was reluctant to change. But now I was not a casual reviewer. It was my responsibility to approve this paper for submission. Though we had sparred before, I was as considerate as I could possibly be in asking him to review how he had arrived at this assumption. Without questioning it, I suggested we go back a few steps in the development and consider what alternative routes one might take. Eventually, we found an only slightly modified assumption that we could both agree upon and I was delighted to approve the release of the paper.

The second concern was over a project my best friend was conducting to develop a new vapor deposition process aimed at enhancing the adhesion of a vaporized metal on a plastic substrate. The project had been going longer than planned and there was no limit to the variables that could be tested. I was afraid the scientist was a perfectionist and would never lock into a process for transfer to the interested business. We agreed that a conversation with the customer was timely. It helped resolve our problem and narrowed the variables that needed testing. I was convinced that my involvement helped bring this project to a successful conclusion much earlier than would otherwise have been the case. There is nothing like talking to the customer.

With those two issues resolved, I was able to begin the more enjoyable task of recruiting two Ph.D.s and one B.S. engineer to bring the section up to full strength. It took a week to review all the resumes obtained from GE visits to chemical engineering departments around the country. Fortunately, I found the people that met our requirements, and a chemical engineering Ph.D. from Illinois came specifically to take over the research I had underway on permeable membranes.

CON-FUSION

For a while, I actually had some time to work in the laboratory, but Art Bueche had another idea in mind. The company had been supporting a research project on fusion-produced electric power and the question was whether this had reached the point of meriting the expansion of effort into a significant development project, or whether it should remain a research project. Art asked me to join the team being created. I had to learn about superconducting magnets and powerful RF generators, and high-energy plasma—all of which confirmed that I should have taken more college physics courses. Nevertheless, the other scientists and I, under the manager of strategic planning for the laboratory, completed this project in four months and made our presentation to the director and his department chiefs.

Our conclusion was that if no new instabilities were discovered in the plasma as its energy and density increased to the fusion level, then it was worthwhile to begin engineering development of an expensive pilot plant. Unfortunately, shortly after our report, another instability problem was discovered and the Research Lab director, Dr. C. Guy Suits, concluded that it was too early for expansion of the program. How wise he was. Fifty years later, the experiments have gotten much larger and more instabilities are being found. I was glad I was not a plasma physicist.

When one study would finish, Art would usually have another for me to take on. I was learning with each new project and becoming familiar with multiple general managers throughout the company.

Meanwhile, one of the chemical engineers was developing a process to make the monomer for a new polymer being pursued by GE Plastics. This project, in Pittsfield, Mass., was being managed by Jack Welch, the same Illinois Ph.D. candidate I had interviewed and brought to the company the year before. Now, he was managing the pilot plant to make the polymer known as poly(p-phenylene oxide), or PPO. Our job in the GE Research Lab was concentrated on the catalytic reaction to make the new monomer. No matter what results our scientist would obtain, Jack would want more—higher yields, longer life, and so on. I learned that for an aggressive manager, "good is not enough." I began to appreciate what the Illinois professors had told me—that Jack was an outstanding leader. Within a year, he was to become the PPO program manager.

This project brought me in contact with Jack's boss, Reuben Gutoff, head of the Plastics Department. He was a most entrepreneurial manager and had heard about a higher-temperature polymer than PPO that was dubbed P3O. The monomer from which this polymer would be produced was being manufactured at a plant in Scotland, based on a license from a French government laboratory on the edge of Paris. Reuben asked me to join two of his business development managers on a trip to visit both the research institute in Paris, as well as the plant in Scotland. This would be my first trip overseas, and I even bought a new attaché case to be appropriately equipped.

By day, we worked hard unraveling the economics of the French process and negotiating terms of a potential agreement. By night, we explored Paris. After four days, we flew to London, took a train to northern Scotland, saw the plant, confirmed that the process worked, and had time for one night back in London. The three of us saved money by crowding into one hotel bedroom and walking in the cities wherever we went. It was one special assignment I immensely enjoyed. Unfortunately, as happens in the majority of such cases, the project did not work out. But Reuben appreciated that we had done a good job in evaluating the monomer process. That was not what killed the project.

NEW LEADERSHIP

Meanwhile, rumors were flying that Guy Suits, the head of the Research Laboratory, was about to retire. Eventually, an official notice of his retirement was issued, coupled with an announcement that Art Bueche would become head of the entire Research Laboratory. The word was that Art was the best-prepared staff member reporting to Dr. Suits. I really felt I had contributed to Art's success with the work I had done on the many studies he had assigned to me.

This leadership change resulted in an opening for someone to head the Chemistry Department. I recognized that with five experienced section managers, who had been in their jobs much longer than I, there was little chance I would be chosen. Also, I did not feel ready for that position. However, in the restructuring of the sections under the new Chemistry Department manager, I did find my job responsibilities doubling in size. The manager of the Combustion and Fluid Dynamics section retired and, rather than appoint a successor, Bueche combined that section with the Chemical Engineering section, suddenly expanding my group to 15 scientists.

One of the scientists reporting to me had developed a theory on how a two-phase mixture of liquid hydrogen and gaseous hydrogen would behave inside the fuel tank of a huge Saturn rocket. He was funded by a NASA contract, and the Apollo Project was counting on his theory. In this case, I found he had good answers to my toughest questions. I began to appreciate the difficulty of the problem and why NASA had given GE the contract. The two of us traveled to Huntsville, Ala., so that he could present his work and perhaps get a bigger contract. I still felt badly about the scientist whose theory I had unraveled years ago, but was pleased to have helped enhance this scientist's presentation by the quizzing I had given him.

Approximately once a year, we would have an annual review where individual scientists would present their work to the Chemistry Department staff. We worked extra hard on these reports and the morning of the presentation, the department staff gave each of the scientists a "We Try Harder" lapel pin that I had picked up at an Avis rental counter. The department staff had to admit that it was justified.

As I became comfortable in my managerial role, I could not help but recognize that the upward opportunities did not look very good. The lab managers were all pure scientists, not engineers. Art Bueche was only 45 years old and had a good 20 years before retirement. Should I stay in my current job, which was very satisfying and would probably become easier with more experience, or should I be looking for a position in which GE engineers had a better chance of getting promoted? I'm not sure if I suggested it to anyone in management, but in any case, after being the Chemical Engineering manager for 3½ years, Art Bueche called me to ask if I would be interested in interviewing to become the manager for R&D in the Silicone Products business in nearby Waterford, N.Y. I couldn't have found a better opportunity. The business was growing and profitable. Moreover, the R&D section was huge compared to my research group. Obviously, I had to interview with the general manager, but in only a few days I had the position. I knew a little bit about the silicone business because the first permeable membranes I used were composed of silicone rubber. But I had never taken the time to learn the chemistry of how the rubber was produced. Fortunately, a very experienced silicone chemist, Al Gilbert, worked in the Research Lab and, one afternoon, gave me a crash course on silicone chemistry.

With trepidation, I said my adieus to the Research Lab scientists, but assured them I would be back asking for breakthroughs in silicone chemistry once I found what was needed.

CONCLUSIONS

1. It is my observation, today, that the first level of management is often the most poorly defined and most demanding of any of the jobs in business.

2. Your job objectives are usually subjective, not quantitative nor objective. They will often be changed by higher-level managers.

3. Your employees, all individual contributors, are less experienced and need more guidance, both with regards to their work and their personal development. Many of them are in transition from academia to industry and you are their mentor.

4. Many times, you are still expected to perform some of your previous tasks (*e.g.*, I continued my membrane research briefly). Generally, this is not a good idea. Some first-time managers do it in case they do not succeed as a manager. When things get tough, it's too easy to go back to the bench—not an entrepreneurial approach to a promotion. Having hired a scientist to take over that membrane project made my transition to full-time manager easy.

5. Your learning requirements expand significantly as you attempt to become knowledgeable in all the different areas being pursued by people working under you. Be selective in where you put your early efforts. Don't waste time where problems don't exist.

6. On being appointed to your first management position, be very modest and appreciative of the opportunity. Spend time with each employee who reports to you and you will find a wide disparity in styles and capabilities. Decide who needs help the most, who is the most difficult to analyze or communicate with, and who is beyond help. Hopefully there will be very few in the latter category; ask your HR organization to assist in dealing with them.

7. Talk to your peers. What do they think of your team? Are there opportunities for more coordination and cooperation? What did your peers learn when they were appointed managers? Where could you and your team be helpful to them?

8. After a month or two, put together your initial assessments and plans for the next year. Then make a date with your boss, who will be very interested to hear your conclusions. Ask for his/her feedback on your assessments and how your plan fits into his/her strategies. This will hopefully please him and confirm his brilliance in selecting you for the new position. You will be off to a great start.

9. You are responsible for the sustainability of your work group. The families of your subordinates are counting on you for the success of their loved one's job. Are you selling your team's capabilities in order to be given the necessary, continued corporate financial support? Are you looking for new customers? Do the members of your group have the right skills to make your efforts successful? The latter is perhaps your first priority.

10. Never get too relaxed. Never stop thinking about what else you can do to achieve more than is expected.

ADVICE TO DEPARTMENT MANAGERS: Every time you appoint a new unit manager, you run two risks: first is ruining a good individual contributor who is not ready for such a transition; second is jeopardizing the optimal functioning of the existing group without that individual.

This is an opportunity to examine the existing structure of the unit involved. Should it be dissolved or expanded through transfers in or out? Should the focus of the work change? Rarely is replacing the unit manager with a "twin" the best solution. Don't waste this opportunity to make any change you believe should be implemented.

In addition, you probably have unit managers on their first managerial assignments. They have probably never had a course on "management," so you must be their mentor. Attack apparent weaknesses very quickly. Sense and address the concerns that bother the new managers. Remember that they are taking a major risk, leaving individual jobs where they were successful, to take on whole new lists of responsibilities. They could very possibly now be managing one of their personal friends as well as one of their closest competitors. Are you or an HR specialist having bi-weekly discussions with new managers during their initial months on the job?

Consider your most seasoned managers to act as mentors to your newest managers. It is likely the managers-in-training will reveal their concerns more readily to peers than to the department manager.

Lastly, insist that young managers look at their peers as partners within the department team and not as competitors for your job.

Chapter 5

Taking Risks as an R&D Manager

LEAVING THE GE RESEARCH LAB, with 25 people in my organization, to move to GE Silicone Products as R&D manager, was quite a significant transition. My new group was composed of 100 chemists and chemical engineers, plus another 100 technicians and pilot plant operators. Moreover, GE Silicone Products was a $36 million business, very high tech, and growing. I would be on the department staff reporting to the general manager. I knew only two of the unit managers, and they knew me only through my research using silicone membranes several years earlier. The general manager of Silicone Products had assembled the R&D unit managers at 8 a.m. on a Monday in April, 1965. When I walked into the conference room with him, their collective chins dropped. I was probably the last person they had expected to see as their new section manager. Moreover, I had no idea how to start the meeting as my new boss left the room.

I knew so little about the business, the technology, or what their issues might be, that saying anything about their business would only make me look foolish. So I told them they would have plenty of time to bring me up to speed and I could hardly wait to learn about each unit's issues and opportunities. But, to start, I thought it would be worth their knowing more about me than what they knew about "Walt Robb, the membrane scientist." Also, it would help show where I was coming from.

I began by explaining that the chemical engineering group at the GE Research Lab rarely got into projects without an identified interest from a GE business. I regretted that we never had a project to help GE Silicone Products. Then I described the new polymer project that Jack Welch was leading in the plastics business and how one of our scientists was developing the process for making the monomer used to make PPO. I was surprised they were not more knowledgeable about a new polymer being developed in another GE business and remarked that one of my goals would be to increase our knowledge about what was going on in GE Plastics.

I mentioned another project with the GE Major Appliances business to develop a better urethane foam insulation for refrigerators and about my earlier work with GE Lighting and the Carboloy businesses regarding tungsten processing. Beyond the chemical field, I discussed another scientist's project on jet engine combustors to improve fuel utilization. Also, GE's work with NASA on the behavior of mixtures of gas and liquid hydrogen in a rocket provided a take-off point for my discussion on getting government R&D contracts.

I covered several other projects that further amplified the diversity of the Lab's chemical engineering research unit that they knew little about. It also illustrated that I was no longer a scientist who would be diving deeply into their responsibilities. Rather, I was accustomed to senior scientists being responsible for their own work. I was there to help, not direct. I would be their liaison on the department staff and they could be certain that I would promote the importance of R&D and all the good things they were doing for the business. I would fight for R&D money to fund projects that the business desired, but I would also take on the job of selling to management their new ideas that might have not gotten strong support in the past.

The review gave them a new appreciation about what I had been doing at the Research Lab and, I believe, was far more beneficial than my saying anything about the silicone business. We then set up a schedule for me to visit each unit manager in his office, followed by a tour of his labs. I also made sure that there were no critical issues that required my immediate attention.

Lastly, I talked about my enthusiasm for being part of a product business. While a central laboratory was vital to the company's ongoing efforts, in a business "you shoot real bullets." I was excited to hear the challenges that the research group faced and was eager to help make GE Silicone Products grow. I was very pleased with how the morning went.

INTEGRATING R&D

After a week spent getting acquainted with each unit manager and his team, learning some of the "lingo" which was characteristic of the business, I spent a part of the following week visiting the other section managers who made up the department staff. They also were surprised the new R&D section manager had not come from the silicone industry. And, while I did not give them an account of my past laboratory activities, I did emphasize about how excited I was about all aspects of the business and how important was the integration of R&D with manufacturing, marketing, and even sales. Then I emphasized that I was visiting them to learn how R&D could better serve the department from their standpoint. This piqued their interest and was well received. Their response confirmed my suspicion that R&D had been too much of an island in the business. Insuring that what we were doing matched what they needed was going to become an important part of my job. At the end of that week, I attended my first department staff meeting. Several section managers told me that my visit to their offices was the first time an R&D manager had ever stepped into their areas. In time, many of them would visit my office, but much more frequently, I went to theirs.

Over the next several months, the business spent important weeks on strategic planning, and out of this came the 10 key R&D projects that Marketing and Sales were counting on for the next year's growth. I made sure that the work schedule for the chemists and engineers was consistent with what the business needed. We did not always make the schedule, but it was not for lack of trying. I did not want to have any "surprises." Fortunately, the marketing people realized that a good relationship between us was extremely important. Too often, Marketing was looking for one set of specifications, while R&D was hoping to get by with less difficult ones. I was pleased that good cooperation was developing between our two functions.

NURTURING EXISTING TALENT

The head of the chemical engineering unit at GE Silicone Products, who had earlier succeeded me as president of the Capital Region Section of the American Institute of Chemical Engineers, was doing an outstanding job. His supervisory functions were over two very different areas: process research and directing a pilot plant. I soon began to wonder why he had not been given the section management assignment. Though he knew more about the business than anyone, he was reticent to speak up in a confrontational environment. So I began working with him to increase his self-confidence. Whenever I was required to be away from the office, I took the risk to recommend him as my back-up, giving him more exposure to the general manager than he ever had before.

After a year on the job, I assessed that the chemists were too narrowly focused and would benefit from an in-house advanced chemistry course that they could attend for two hours a week from 4-6 p.m. Outside speakers covered areas they knew little or nothing about. The chemists loved it and did not mind staying the extra hour each week to attend. I felt rewarded for taking the risk to schedule that course.

While I never got intimately involved with the many technical projects underway, I greatly enjoyed representing the R&D section at the monthly staff meetings. The general manager, an outstanding former sales manager, believed in full participation of the functional managers in every major decision process; this even carried over to setting of the sales budget for the upcoming year. At a half-day staff meeting dedicated to budgetary deliberation for 1967, we had a thorough discussion of the year's forecast. The sales manager bragged that next year we would achieve an 11% increase over the previous year. While better than the previous forecast, we all felt the business had the momentum, along with new unbudgeted products, to do much better. The GM said we would arrive at the sales budget by averaging our individual forecasts, which at the time seemed very considerate of him. Of course, we knew that the higher the budget for next year, the more expense money each of us would get for our sections. As a result, our forecast for the next year, in spite of some economists predicting a significant slowing in the domestic economy, was for a 10% sales increase. The GM responded, "OK, but now you have to make it happen." He would have been happier budgeting half of that sales growth.

As it happened, sales increased only 6%, a significant budget miss. I decided that if I became a GM, I would not let my staff members sway my judgment with their overly enthusiastic optimism.

HONING MANAGEMENT SKILLS

After I had been R&D manager for two years, I was invited to take the GE General Management Course customarily given to well-performing section level managers. Thirty of us from throughout General Electric would be spending thirteen weeks at the company's professional education center in Crotonville, N.Y., a 2½-hour drive from home for me. This meant that I could get home with my growing family of three sons each weekend, not practical for the students from the West Coast. I recommended to the Silicone Products general manager that the Chemical Engineering unit manager be appointed as the interim R&D manager, thus continuing his development. We lived near each other and talked by phone during the week and in person on weekends.

Fortunately, there were no problems that distracted me from the course and I found it to be a jam-packed, MBA-level program concentrating on managing a business at General Electric. The sales and marketing managers in the class were sure that they were on their way to becoming business general managers. That feeling wasn't shared among the other functional managers in the class and this bothered me immensely. I decided, for the first time, that I had the potential to be a business general manager and resolved to do something about it.

A NEW OPPORTUNITY APPEARS

Shortly after returning to the business, I was scheduled for my annual manpower review with the GM. The review went well and my boss was delighted I had been willing to leave the Research

Laboratory for Silicone Products. He noted the R&D section was coupled to the business more closely than ever before. Then I took the risk of asking him to recommend me as a GM of a GE business at some future time. I still remember his response: "Walt, you have never gotten an order. You have never made a sales call. But, relax, you are a doing a great job as R&D manager." I did not make a fuss about his comments, but I did note my request in the interview summary sheet, and started looking at where I might go outside of General Electric.

One of the great things about GE is that summaries of manpower discussions are forwarded to the next level of management. About two months after my review, I received a call from Reuben Gutoff, who had gotten to know me when I was at the Research Lab doing due diligence on a new polymer that he was considering commercializing. He was, by this time, promoted from head of the Plastics business to Vice President and Division General Manager of the Chemical and Medical Division. His opening remark regarding my desire to become a GM told me that he had read the "write-up" from my manpower review. He asked how strongly I felt about becoming a general manager and I told him that I was considering looking outside GE for advancement, if that was the way technical leaders were perceived in the company. I knew I had an ally, since he was a chemical engineer who had become a GE general manager. Now under him were the various material businesses in the company, the medical x-ray business, and the Chemical Development Operations (CDO). This operation had been the developer of new polymers for the company, with Lexan® polycarbonate being CDO's big winner.

Reuben told me that the company's strategic planning team had been pleased with the way CDO had helped the material business and proposed that he form a Medical Development Operations (MDO). This would be an incubator for medical businesses separate from the x-ray imaging business. The specific idea was for GE to acquire an automated clinical laboratory, a number of which already existed in the country, growing out of an automated blood analyzer made by an instrument company called Technicon.

Reuben said that he had money in his budget to cover my expenses, along with a secretary and market researcher. His legal counsel would also have time to be very supportive to me. The level was not quite that of a general manager, but it was more than a section manager and had potential. I could see how he had gone from being the general manager of CDO to becoming a company vice president. I was willing to take a chance as an "operations" manager if that was required on the way to becoming a GM. Heading a clinical laboratory was not my first choice, but it was a risk I was willing to take.

Initially, this position would require moving my office next to his in Bridgeport, Conn., but I would be doing lots of traveling and occasionally visiting the GE Research Lab in the evaluation of clinical laboratory technologies. That insured I would at least get home on weekends. Moreover, Bridgeport was only a temporary office until we acquired a laboratory.

I regretted having to go back to Silicone Products and announce that I was leaving, but was delighted that the staff and GM agreed that the Chemical Engineering manager had evolved into an excellent replacement.

While much had happened over those three years at Silicone Products that would not be described as "entrepreneurial," nonetheless, compared to my predecessor, my activities were seen just that way. My partnership with the other staff managers, my strong participation in business management, my study of competitors, my development of a successor, my establishment of a course in advanced chemistry, and my tracking of progress on key projects were, in retrospect, very entrepreneurial. Now, with Reuben Gutoff, I knew I would be working with one of the most entrepreneurial officers in General Electric.

CONCLUSIONS

FOR FIRST-TIME SECTION MANAGERS: As a manager of managers, I found a section manager's position a breeze compared to being a first-level manager. Sometimes, I had to search for risks to take, since my team was so professional and experienced, most having been in their current positions for 10 years or more.

What I attempted was to shake them out of their comfort zones, pushing them to do things faster and more efficiently than had been the practice. We also both terminated and initiated more programs than had been the routine, held "brainstorming" sessions for new ideas, gave more recognition to accomplishments, and, above all, coordinated more partnerships with functions in the business.

In retrospect, I wonder if I might have looked for a more entrepreneurial GM for whom to work. Three years earlier, I had been so anxious to be an R&D manager that I grabbed the first opportunity that came along. It worked out all right, but I was disappointed that I had not found opportunities to take as many risks as I would have liked.

FOR GENERAL MANAGERS: There is nothing wrong with being a conservative general manager; some businesses require such an approach. But when one hires staff managers with entrepreneurial desires, it needs to be recognized that to make the most efficient use of such persons, while keeping them happy and challenged, requires some additional effort on your part. Discuss upfront with your managers the reasons for the conservative strategies you are pursuing. At the same time, listen to their risky proposals. They may actually be well worth implementing. In the end, though, you are responsible

For example, can a manager come up with ways to reduce inventory, stretch accounts payable, or shrink receivables to conserve cash? Can an R&D manager suggest a more effective advertising plan at lower cost? What about ideas to make R&D more effective in either development time or lower cost?

At the same time, give them warning that ideas like making an acquisition or starting a new business function would have a difficult time fitting into the budget the company has for the business. But there is no next year. Remind them that the first priority of the business is to make the budget.

Chapter 6

Taking Risks as a Start-Up Manager

ON A SUNDAY NIGHT in April, 1968, I drove to Bridgeport, Conn., just to insure that as manager of the new Medical Development Operations (MDO), I would be on time for my 8 a.m. kick-off meeting with Reuben Gutoff, V.P. and General Manager of the Chemical and Medical Division. Reuben wanted to demonstrate that start-ups could still succeed in a huge corporation like General Electric. He had the mandate from the company's strategic planning committee to explore the feasibility of GE entering a new, rapidly growing business in automated clinical laboratories. Technicon Corporation had triggered a revolution in clinical laboratories by commercializing an automated blood analyzer capable of performing 20 different analyses on a blood sample in just one minute. These machines were so efficient that both private doctors and hospitals were sending their blood samples to independent laboratories equipped with these devices. Some clinical laboratories also did additional tests that were not as automated, such as tissue samples, but the bulk of the business was blood testing. Samples would be picked up by laboratory couriers one day and the analyses reported the next. Yes, I was really taking a risk with this assignment, but it seemed feasible and the potential rewards were great.

We were aware of five private laboratories that were potential candidates for our acquisition effort. We agreed that acquiring an existing laboratory would be far more efficient that starting another from scratch.

SEARCHING OUT TECHNOLOGY

I set about studying the report prepared by the GE strategic planning committee, as well as a book on health care that Reuben presented to me as a memento of this kick-off. Over the next several days, I talked to company doctors and acquaintances, looking for anyone who had experience with an automated laboratory. None did, relying instead on old-fashioned hospital laboratories. At least that gave me encouragement that the market was only starting to develop. A call to the Research Lab struck gold where a scientist, having heard about GE's clinical interest, had used his knowledge of fuel cells to invent an instrument that could measure the "catalyze enzyme concentration" in urine. The primary market was expected to be women, for whom a urinary tract infection is especially difficult. I loved the fact that I now had something invented at GE that I could use as an excuse to visit laboratories.

My next trip was forty miles west of Bridgeport to visit Technicon. My excuse was to inquire if they had any interest in an automated urine analyzer and, if so, were they interested in licensing a newly developed enzyme test.

Of course, we also discussed the Automated Sequence Analyzer (ASA), the name for Technicon's blood analyzer. I learned that it relied on membranes to separate components in the blood for many of the tests. Now, I had another area where GE could make a contribution and where my membrane research experience would be useful.

After several weeks of study, including a European trip to Brussels with Reuben and the general manager of the X-Ray Department, Walt Nelson, I now knew a lot more about the medical business. It also was clear that Walt had no interest in the clinical lab business and would be just as happy if the project disappeared.

I was introduced to a leading European pathologist in Brussels who spoke English and knew all about Technicon. However, he was more interested in having his own analyzer than in sending blood samples to an outside laboratory. Saving money on the cost of blood tests was of no concern to him.

A PLAN ABORTED

Back in the U.S., I began visiting private laboratories, primarily inquiring as to their interest in catalyze testing or membranes for their own development of new blood tests. I inquired casually about their interest in being acquired and usually got a qualified yes. The exception was when I visited King's County Laboratory in Brooklyn. This laboratory, owned by the Blavis family, was growing sales at about 30% per year following their acquisition of a Technicon ASA machine. Current annual sales were $3 million processing some 150,000 samples, primarily from clinics and small hospitals. They were very concerned that most competitive laboratories had wider expertise than King's County Lab. While they were nicely profitable, they were ready to take cash for the business and retire.

A few days later, I learned that a competitive lab was being acquired by a pharmaceutical company and heard a rumor that another had been offered $7.5 million for their business. The Blavises were convinced that they were the pioneers in automated testing and were the fastest growing laboratory. Therefore, they felt strongly that King's County Lab was worth $8 million.

I got to know their brilliant lawyer who had an office in the skyscraper over Grand Central Station. He let me know that the Blavises were willing to wait for the right offer. They liked the idea of being acquired by GE, but there was no way they would sell for less than $8 million.

How does one determine what a laboratory is worth? I was able to confirm the sale of another laboratory with similar sales for $7.5 million. In the scheme of things, I could see that maintaining a 30% growth rate would require considerable cash until sales reached $15 million—GE's five-year goal. So, the purchase price itself was not a big obstacle.

I was anxious to consummate the acquisition and sold the GE Review Board on the wisdom of making an offer to the Blavis family. A date was set for a meeting with Mr. and Mrs. Blavis at their lawyer's office. It was important that a GE officer make the offer; Reuben was looking forward to negotiating this purchase. On the way to the meeting, he told me that his boss had given him authorization to pay $6.5 million for the business. I was beside myself and reiterated the strong warning from the Blavis family lawyer. I predicted our efforts would take a tremendous step backwards. Reuben said this was a new experience for me. "Just observe," he counseled.

Reuben made a beautiful speech about how right it was for GE to enter the clinical laboratory field and how the fit with King's County Laboratory was perfect. They would always be proud that they had sold the company to GE and, with the help of our Research Laboratory, we would develop unique tests and keep the lab #1 in the country. He then said, "I am pleased to offer you $6.5 million for the business."

In an instant, the lawyer stood up and slammed a book on his conference table that was like a pistol shot. "Mr. Gutoff," he said, "you have insulted the Blavis family. You have been told that only an $8 million dollar offer would be acceptable. This meeting is over." He led the Blavises out of the room, leaving Reuben and me alone staring after them. I felt my desire to become a business manager had just been shot out from under me, but Reuben assured me, "Relax, they will be back." Unfortunately, that was not the case. Two weeks later, we learned that Hoffman-La Roche had bought King's County Laboratories for $8 million. My risk was for naught.

IN-HOUSE SOLUTION

Recognizing that only having one candidate for an acquisition is not a safe option, and wondering what I might do if the acquisition effort did not succeed, I had kept in contact with Technicon Corporation. While they had no interest in a urine analyzer, they did have an interest in a new source for a carbon-dioxide permeable membrane, a technology I had developed in 1961. It turned out that every ASA analyzer required a carbon-dioxide permeable membrane that had to be replaced once a week. Technicon, as specified in the warranty it supplied with the analyzer, was the only approved consumable supplier, so there was no possibility of competing against them. I did learn that they bought their existing membranes for 50 cents apiece and then resold them to the laboratories for several dollars each. I estimated we could make a nice profit selling them membranes in a cardboard mount for 40 cents each. Technicon loved the cardboard frame and, in no time, gave me a $40,000 order for 100,000 mounts. I was amazed at my selling ability and Technicon's willingness to take a risk on a new business.

With that order in hand, I approached Reuben about setting up a membrane products section in MDO. I put together a business plan that said we could get into a break-even operation with a $100,000 investment. I could see the opportunity for the business growing to a few million dollars as we learned to make other membranes for the ASA machine. Reuben was happy to have something come out of the laboratory acquisition effort and approved the budget for us to get started.

Now I needed a laboratory and factory space, both of which were available in the Schenectady main plant at practically no cost. So, now I could live back home and eliminate the commute to Bridgeport. Marilyn Smith now became my secretary. She later decided to travel and was replaced by Arlene McElroy. The market research intern that I had hired for the lab study became the membrane sales specialist, and I hired a production specialist to be my manufacturing manager. We also gave a little money to the Research Lab for additional testing on the Catalyze Enzyme Analyzer. A year later, several people from the Research Lab joined MDO as part of our research and development arm.

The first full year, we had a sales budget of $150,000 and just barely made it. The next year, we did $450,000 and sales continued to expand as other laboratory instrument manufacturers came to us for specialized membranes. Technicon remained our biggest customer and we were their only supplier. If they only knew how frail their supply chain was! It would have been a disaster for Technicon if we could not match their growing requirements. I'm sure that the GE name made the difference.

As another opportunity for the membrane business, we took information from the work that had been performed on my artificial gill and used it to investigate the development of a membrane lung for humans. Led by an outstanding chemist named Bill Mathewson, the team developed an artificial lung that was able to keep pigs alive by circulating their blood on one side of the permeable membrane and fresh air on the other. At this time, human open-heart surgery used an artificial lung that mixed the patient's blood directly with air, even though it was known that direct contact of blood with oxygen would be deleterious to the red corpuscles. Artificial lung support was satisfactory for an hour or two—good enough for open heart surgery—but not for sustained support for patients with pneumonia or emphysema.

Eventually, the FDA gave us permission to work with a brave pulmonary physician in testing the lung on a woman who was going to die without such support. The test patient had such serious pneumonia that her lungs were filling with fluid. For eight days, our membrane lung kept her alive with no damage to her blood. Antibiotics were clearing up the pneumonia and the experiment was considered a great success. We were ecstatic.

Unfortunately, weaning the patient off the artificial lung proved to be impossible. The micro-bronchi in her lungs had collapsed and stuck together. Pumping air in would not open the minute air passages and she could not survive with the membrane lung disconnected. No one had anticipated this problem.

As a result of this experiment, doctors learned that when a patient is on a membrane lung, it is necessary to pulse air in and out of the lungs, just as if the patient were breathing normally. Unfortunately, GE was not to reap the benefit of this lesson. The company decided that a high percentage of people in enough distress to be connected to a membrane lung would expire, even with the best of treatment, and the "deep pockets" GE would be an irresistible lure for personal injury lawyers.

We contributed GE's patents and know-how in this area to the public domain, allowing several small firms without "deep pockets" to produce copies of the lung. In time, all open-heart surgery and long-term support procedures were to rely on membrane lungs;

no one would think today of mixing air and blood together. This was a second disappointment for me, and I thought about doing a spin-off from GE to develop this business, though the company did not encourage that. Besides, I had found another exciting direction for MDO to explore.

KEEPING THE PEACE

With increasing sales of our membranes, I had the money to hire an extremely bright MBA as my business development manager. He soon discovered an opportunity for MDO related to a new Federal regulation requiring hearing protectors for employees in even moderately noisy factories. Remembering my knowledge about two-part room-temperature vulcanizing (RTV) silicone rubber, I concluded that material would be excellent for molding "personalized hearing protectors." I visualized a two-part package containing an RTV pre-polymer in one part of the package and a reactant and catalyst in the second part. When mixed together they would make enough silicone putty for two cone-shaped plugs, one for each ear. Even at room temperature, the putty would cure to solid silicone rubber in just ten minutes and perfectly conform to the individual's ear canals.

I assigned this "GE start-up" to the MBA and, while his chemical knowledge was sufficient to understand the process I had in mind, he could not conceive of how to make this into a business. Fortunately, Ted Johnson, who was my initial assistant on doing the laboratory acquisition work, saw the potential in this idea. Putting aside what he had been working on, Ted worked with the manufacturing manager of the membrane product section and quickly developed a perfect two-part plastic envelope. It was easy to break the seal between the two components, which allowed an installer to mix the catalysts with the RTV. On opening the package, a "glob" of putty was available to be split into two cones for insertion into the user's ears.

Ted came up with the name "Peacekeepers," and hand-produced material for the initial tests with employees in several General Electric production facilities. The workers loved the comfort of these personalized earplugs and appreciated that the company was not forcing them to wear uncomfortable, non-customized commercial earplugs. And at a cost of just $15 per set, Peacekeepers were well accepted. With the company's endorsement, we looked for an exciting application that would give these earplugs some glamour. We learned that hearing problems were common among pit crews at auto racing events. So Ted, with the help of Reuben Gutoff, identified and signed up the "Voice of Racing," Chris Economaki, a well-known figure with the right connections to racers and racing fans to become our image-maker.

At the next Indianapolis 500 race, Ted and his assistants got permission to be in the infield with a trailer where drivers and their crews could get personalized earplugs made during the pre-race week. We had this filmed and Chris narrated the five-minute movie showing well-known drivers getting their earpieces. There had never been a better promotional film made at less cost. I remembered that someone once told me that R&D managers could not lead marketing programs.

Ted and his team later had an exhibit at a safety equipment show, where our two technicians were busy all day molding personalized earplugs in our booth. Companies understood the advantages of Peacekeepers over the pre-formed earplugs. Within one year, sales were over $1 million and climbing.

We then saw the opportunity to expand the business with a van that would be equipped with audio test equipment. Our staff could pull up to a factory, test the employees' hearing, and either mold Peacekeepers for them or train factory personnel to do it. In a year and a half, the Peacekeeper business had a significant percentage of the new hearing protectors being sold in the country. GE had never seen a product go so quickly from idea to rapid growth and profit as did these earplugs. We were forecasting a $3 million sales rate.

WESTWARD EXPANSION

About this time, Walt Nelson, the head of GE X-Ray, retired and Reuben Gutoff appointed Julien ("Jim") Charlier to replace Nelson. Jim had been the general manager of a small Belgian x-ray manufacturing company that Walt Nelson had acquired a few years earlier. Charlier's expertise was designing x-ray equipment to image different parts of the body. His newest product, which had attracted GE's attention, was a remote-control x-ray system that was produced in his Liege, Belgium, plant. No other x-ray company could match that product. Shortly after Charlier's appointment, the Milwaukee business was renamed "Medical Systems" and soon was upgraded to a GE division. At that time, Reuben was promoted from a division vice president to a group executive. MDO was transferred to the new Medical Systems Department and its name changed to Medical Ventures Operation. I now reported to Jim Charlier.

Charlier moved to Milwaukee and was soon designing new x-ray products for the radiology community. He now had a factory twenty times the size of the one in Liege and loved the opportunity this position afforded him.

As part of the business, he inherited a dental x-ray operation with sales plateaued at $2.5 million per year. It was making a small profit, but could not afford the cost of developing new products. Charlier suggested to Reuben that the dental x-ray business be transferred to the newly-renamed Medical Ventures Operation, thus enabling Charlier to not even think about the dental business. Reuben was glad to have me take an independent look at this stagnant business.

Fortunately, with the profit from the Peacekeeper business, I could now allow the dental business to invest in a new type of dental x-ray scanner that took an image of the entire array of teeth in one long film as a supplement to the normal one-inch "bite-wing" films that covered a couple of teeth at a time. The manager of this business was delighted to be swapping ideas with the entrepreneurial MVO management. Within a year, dental sales had increased to $3 million with income growing even faster.

About this same time, Jim Charlier discovered that radiology departments were starting to buy a new imaging device that, coupled with radioactive technetium-99 injected into the body, could locate the site of cancerous tumors. The device was called a nuclear scanner and GE trailed its primary U.S. competitor, Picker, in not yet having one. Reuben and Jim decided to give me the responsibility for developing or acquiring such a product. I knew a scientist from the Research Laboratory who wanted to be a product manager and was strongly interested in this challenge. Dale Kirkbride had come into MVO with the transfer of the catalyze enzyme detector. While we were trying to find a champion for that instrument, he saw this as a much better opportunity.

In no time, Dale located an Israeli company, called Elscint, which had a nuclear scanner it sold in Europe and Israel, but lacked a U.S. distributor. Dr. Avraham Suhami, Elscint's president, loved the opportunity of having GE distribute his product in the United States. We soon had a prototype installed in a U.S. hospital and found it to be adequate, but in need of some improvement. With Dr. Suhami's commitment to improve the product before beginning commercial shipments, we ordered 10 units. The initial announcement of this product as part of the GE Medical Systems' booth at the huge Radiological Society of North America exhibit in Chicago was scheduled for December 1, 1971. That would be a big event for MVO.

As I looked forward to a couple of days of vacation around Thanksgiving before going to Chicago, I could not help but look back over the past 3½ years and feel very satisfied with what we had accomplished. I had gained a reputation as an entrepreneur and risk-taker and loved what I was doing.

While we did not acquire a clinical laboratory, with barely $250,000 in funding from GE, we had developed two new businesses, enhanced another, and were about to introduce a fourth business in nuclear imaging. Annual sales had reached $7.5 million and we were forecasting $9 million in 1972. MVO was profitable and a likely candidate for departmental status in the company. Though Charlier was giving me good pay increases, I was not thrilled to be reporting to him. We rarely spoke, even for him to compliment me on always being ahead of the sales budget.

On Wednesday evening before Thanksgiving, I got a call from Jack Welch, who had been promoted to head the newly-formed Chemical and Metallurgical Division, following Reuben in that position. Out of the blue, he asked me to meet with him in his home in Pittsfield, Mass., on Friday morning. A holiday meant very little to Jack. I could not imagine what he had in mind.

CONCLUSIONS

FOR A CORPORATE VENTURE MANAGER: You need to face the fact that few large corporations will start an entirely new product business from scratch. The company will instead acquire a start-up or initiate the venture as part of an existing business. My venture operation was totally separate from any of the other GE operations, though I reported to a division manager who was responsible for multiple businesses and a chemical development operation. That was far better than reporting to a typical start-up board. Unfortunately, few companies have a Reuben Gutoff or a Jack Welch in their ranks.

From my experience, I recommend you clarify with your boss the specific expectations for the venture, which may be more than the company or division manager has really documented. The more sketchily it is defined, the more closely you will need to communicate with your boss. Recognize that there is likely no budget for the venture other than for your exploratory expenses. Hopefully, you are initiating such a project during prosperous times for the company. I would not advise becoming a corporate venture manager in an economic downturn.

Expect to take big risks; you are not being given the job to undertake little ones. But be aware that your job may be the first in the division to be cut. Take on the position with some personal money in the bank.

Hire capable people, preferably from inside the company, who are like you: satisfied with the corporation but anxious to be involved in what promises to be a more exciting and more rewarding opportunity. Like you, they are willing to take risks. You do not need detractors.

Ask for advice from friends in the company beyond your boss. They will probably think you are crazy, but it helps to get their independent thoughts. It is better to have a critic as a friend than an employee.

Put 90% of your effort into the main thrust of the venture and 10% in a "lifeboat" project in case the main effort proves unsuccessful. For me, that was the membrane business.

Chapter 7

Taking Risks as a New General Manager

BY LATE 1971, Jack Welch, the Illinois graduate student I had brought into GE ten years before, was now GE's youngest division manager with six materials departments reporting to him. I couldn't wait to hear what he had to discuss.

After coffee and a few minutes of small talk, Jack told me that he had just fired the general manager of GE's silicone business, located in Waterford, N.Y. This is where I had been the R&D manager 3½ years earlier, just before taking up the Medical Venture Operation challenge. I knew the business, but barely knew the general manager who came after I had left. I did know that GE had considered it a growth business, but sales, unfortunately, had plateaued for two years at $47 million. Jack's exact words were, "I would like you to become the GM at Silicone Products. It's already cleared with Julien Charlier."

MOVING ON UP

Finally, I was going to become a general manager and with a business I already knew something about. So I immediately said, 'Yes, I'm ready to go. How soon can I start?' He replied, "How about Monday? The former GM has found another job in the company and has cleared out his desk. His secretary will be expecting you. Also, I hope your favorite direct report in the

Medical Ventures Operations will be happy to take your place. Congratulations on having him ready to take over."

Jack continued, "Your sales budget for next year is $48.5 million, a modest 3% increase, and you need to get the business back to making a 10% net profit. What I want you to do above all else is teach the business how to make a budget."

I agreed, knowing the opportunities in the business when I was there should make this a reasonable target. I also felt comfortable that if I should discover too much bad news on arriving, I would have a chance to renegotiate with Jack on the budget, if necessary.

As I drove back to Schenectady, I wondered if I had been foolish to accept this new position, when there was so much opportunity still remaining with the Medical Ventures Operation. While the unit was still an "operation," not a department, it had grown from $0 to $7.5 million in sales in 3½ years, and we had a long-range plan that would get revenues to $30 million in five more years. Then it would surely be called a department and I would become a "general manager"—a title with so much more panache than "operation manager." I was getting a good reputation for being an unusual entrepreneur in a huge company. Would I have as much fun with a silicone business that had just come through two years with no growth?

Perhaps the deciding reason for my quick, positive response to Jack was the fact that one year before, MVO had been transferred from the Chemical and Materials Division to the Medical Systems Division, where it was a pimple on the $100 million x-ray imaging business. Jim Charlier, the division head, was so involved with his restructuring of that business that he never spent 10 minutes on MVO. That's a problem for "start-ups" in big corporations.

You would think I would love the independence I had as the MVO manager. But a person likes to be appreciated and recognized, and I was feeling more like Rodney Dangerfield than an entrepreneur.

In any case, I was very excited about reporting to Jack, wherever he wanted to position me.

ACCEPTING THE CHALLENGE

On the Monday morning following Thanksgiving, I was back at the silicone business that I had left not long before. At my new office, the long-time secretary, Kay Saunders, had everything ready for me to sit down and start working. Apparently, an internal press release to the employees had already gone out. There had been rumors that a managerial change was imminent, so no one seemed surprised when I appeared. Jack did not need to introduce me.

The prior general manager of the business gave me a call to wish me well. It was a difficult call, knowing he was not very happy about being replaced. I thanked him for the team he was passing on to me. Eight of the ten people who reported to me had been there before, but there was a new sales manager, Dave Korb, who had been in GE Plastics for a few years before being appointed sales manager for the silicone business 18 months earlier. I was anxious to meet him.

In a meeting with my new staff, I was alerted to two problems that Jack had not mentioned. The first had to do with an expectation by the management team that Dow Corning would soon announce a 10% reduction in the price of silicone fluid, a very major piece of our business. When the silicone business started in 1950, silicone fluid was a new product for both Dow Corning and GE and was priced at $3.00 per pound. Dow Corning, with twice our share of the market, was the product leader. Every year, a few weeks before Christmas, they would announce a price decrease that was intended to encourage new applications for silicone fluid. By 1971, the price had come down to $1.00 per pound. Sure enough, on December 10, Dow announced in the trade journal that the price of fluid would be reduced to $0.90 per pound. Unfortunately, that took most of the profit right out of that segment of our business, not a great way to start the New Year.

We were at an off-site staff meeting when the news arrived. The entire staff, including Dave Korb, told me we had no options but to match this price decrease. If we did not, our silicone fluid sales would drop precipitously. In response to my question regarding the impact of a 10% price decrease on new applications, the staff believed that the positive impact would be small. At $1.00, most buyers believed they were already getting a valuable product. No one believed that a price decrease would expand the market, only take out our profit.

I resisted the full decrease and, counter to my team's recommendations, decided to announce a price drop to $0.95 per pound. It was a huge risk, but I had been taking such risks for years now and my team had to get used to that. A press release went out the next day. The sales force thought I was crazy.

Within a week, Dow Corning was acknowledging that their price would only drop to $0.95 per pound. That was a huge victory for me. Moreover, by improving plant productivity, we could maintain our product margin. (As a footnote, $0.95 per pound was the lowest price that silicone fluid ever reached. The following December, Dow's traditional announcement of a price decrease was never made.)

THREAT FROM WITHIN

The second crisis involved unionization. For 20 years, the hourly workers had been members of an IUE union that had gotten along well with department management. The union members did have some pay advantages, such as larger annual income raises than the non-exempt lab technicians received. Now, these non-exempt employees had been sold on signing a petition to join the union. It was a big win for the IUE and could have been the first step towards unionizing the engineers as well.

I immediately informed Jack of the situation and he appreciated that the timing was very unfortunate. He assigned his human resources specialist to work with the Silicone Products team to, hopefully, win the election scheduled for January 15. We did get the election delayed for 30 days due to the management change. During the next two months, we learned a lot about the many regulations that restrict management activities during the "quiet" period for a union election. Forty years later, it is hard to recall all the details, but we felt that we had convinced the technicians that they had more to gain staying independent than joining the union. Our HR manager for non-exempt employees, Ed Trager, was the person primarily responsible for our communication program and he did everything we were allowed to do. Jack and I had our fingers crossed that the tide toward unionization had been reversed.

On February 15, the voting concluded at 4:00 p.m. Ten minutes later, Ed walked into my office and I sensed immediately that we had lost. Neither of us was used to losing, except in sports, so we hugged and shed a few tears, knowing this was not a very good development for either of our careers. This was a risk I hadn't anticipated. Had I really made the right choice in leaving MVO?

My call to inform Jack of the results was not easy, but it had to be done. It was made somewhat easier because his HR specialist had already given him the news. What really hurt was that we had lost by just one vote out of the 100 cast. To Jack's credit, he was mild in his criticism. He said that the important thing was to put it behind us and run the business so well that the technicians would be sorry they had unionized. I was grateful for his reaction. Today, those workers are still in the union, but not the engineers.

While this was going on, I was also spending the most enjoyable part of each day talking to my sales manager, Dave Korb. I knew that he would be very important to my success, so I wasted no time in getting to know him and hearing his take on what was happening in the marketplace.

I learned that our main competitor, Dow Corning, had twice our market share. Their huge lead over GE was partly due to a large, distributor-based distribution system that gave them excellent nationwide coverage.

We had 50 direct salesmen that we claimed called on every smokestack. However, with only 50 representatives in the entire country, it obviously was not as effective as having 50 distributors with a probable average of five sales representatives each. Dave told me that during the previous year, GE Silicone Products had begun to install a distributor system of its own, but my predecessor had been reluctant to give it the full management attention and backing that it needed.

With my buy-in, Dave was able to launch a distributor incentive program over the following nine months that would culminate in an all-expense-paid appreciation trip to Acapulco, Mexico. A distributor could earn one seat on the chartered flight for every $50,000 in orders they placed with GE. There was a limit of four seats per distributor; we expected them to be filled by their two top managers and their spouses, though any of their employees were eligible. With 50 distributors, we anticipated up to 200 guests. The only element missing was a kick-off meeting to announce the program and get the distributors excited.

I told Dave that if we were going to do this, it had to be done with gusto. I also knew for such a kick-off event to be effective, it would cost more than what was budgeted. But this was the kind of entrepreneurial activity that had great potential to help get the business back on a winning track.

Dave planned the kick-off event for a convention center in the St. Louis area, and engaged Maritz Research, a well-experienced specialist in corporate incentive programs, to manage the event. This was a totally new experience for me, and I was delighted to see how well Maritz worked with us, complete with having movies of the excitement to be enjoyed in Acapulco. We left the kick-off with high expectations, pleased that all 50 distributors had either attended in person or sent a representative.

Sales took off immediately and by year-end, 200 tickets had been earned, just as we planned.

While all the distributors made certain to purchase the $200,000 minimum to earn their four seats, we were especially pleased that some ordered far more material than the program required. As a result, the division did $67 million in sales that year, shattering our $48.5 million budget. It was a huge win for GE.

But that was only part of the excitement. The plant also had to somehow produce 43% more product than it had shipped the previous year. Bob Hatch, our manufacturing manager, welcomed the challenge. Since there was no time to install new capital equipment, the gain in production had to be achieved by stretching the output of the plant far beyond what it had ever done before. While such a sudden jump in production can sometime raise product costs, due to such factors as increased overtime, we actually realized a net reduction in the cost of goods per pound.

Jack was overjoyed. Even though Silicone Products represented only about 12% of total sales in his division, our performance greatly contributed to the overall profit numbers. Reg Jones, who had become the GE CEO by that time and was not optimistic that I was ready for this job, was amazed. Better still, no one brought up the union election results anymore.

We estimated our U.S. market share increased as much as 5% on top of our customary 25% slice. Years later, we were pleased to learn that Dow Corning was not happy.

A LESSON IN HUMILITY

By the end of the second quarter in 1972, it was apparent that sales and product margins were both exceeding the budget. If needed, we felt the business could stretch its historical 10% net return to as much as 15% for the year. Jack cautioned me about such a large jump in percent net income since it could not be expected to occur very often. Rather, he suggested that we should use this bonus income to improve the business for the long term. This allowed us to increase our R&D funding of future products, while expanding our advertising to gain additional sales. We even commissioned a movie about GE Silicone Products and how we were helping "Bring good things to life." Though it's hard to believe now, the film was titled *Love Is the Answer*.

In January of 1973, we had a celebration for the expanded staff that almost got out of control. A local district sales manager, driving home after too much good cheer, ran off the road and wrecked his car. Fortunately, no one was hurt.

What happened to me that night was different, though equally embarrassing. Around midnight, the department lawyer told me he had ordered a taxi to take me home, which I recognized was good advice. You can imagine my chagrin the next morning when I had to ask my wife to drive me to the restaurant to retrieve my car. It was a hard lesson that never had to be repeated. We all learned from that incident, fortunately without anyone getting hurt.

That party was only for the top two levels of management; we decided to reward the sales force and key managers in other parts of the business with a sales meeting in Vail, Colo. This was planned for the peak of their snow season, and a total of 100 employees received slightly risqué invitations to attend the sales meeting. That got us into trouble with some wives—another lesson learned.

In late 1972, our fear was that the distributors were loading up their warehouses with purchases beyond what they might expect to sell in the near future, and that 1973 would be a down year. We still budgeted $78 million, up from the $67 million in sales just accomplished. But Dave assured me that, if distributors saw stuff in their warehouses that wasn't moving, they would push salesmen to get it sold. And apparently, that was the case, because we started the New Year with continued growth.

SOARING TO NEW HEIGHTS

Our annual sales meeting occurred in a very positive atmosphere. Jack was invited and readily accepted. He even asked us to invite his boss, Group Executive Reuben Gutoff. With Reuben's help, we also got Jim McKay, the ABC sports commentator from the 1968 and 1972 Olympics, as a speaker. He had become famous for his commentaries from Munich during the Israeli athlete kidnappings.

I gave a kick-off talk at the beginning of the Monday morning meeting. Jack spoke on Monday night, Reuben the following evening, and McKay starred on Wednesday night.

We scheduled educational meetings each morning and skiing in the afternoons. All but two of the hundred or so people attending took to the slopes, only one of whom suffered an injury the entire time. The event was a huge success for the sales staff and employees alike. And Jack and Reuben were able to see for themselves the new level of esprit in the business after my first year in charge. We also set a record for the largest sales meeting to that time in Vail's short history. It was a win-win-win for everyone.

In April, we took the 200 distributor guests, plus 30 GE managers and spouses to act as hosts, to Acapulco. There were morning business meetings for the distributors and shopping trips for the spouses, but the afternoons were devoted to the beach. A favorite activity was bargaining with the native vendors selling their handicrafts. At dinner, people would show off their purchases and brag about the low prices they paid. One salesman had purchased a two-foot long, three-masted schooner model for $15. That became the new challenge and by the last dinner someone had obtained one for only $3.

The final morning, we announced our next incentive program would be to the Costa del Sol on the southern coast of Spain. Again, we had movies to highlight the wonderful attractions of the resort that we all hoped to visit.

Although many of the people had suffered short bouts of gastric distress, everyone considered the event a great success. We and our distributors felt like a family, eager to take on Dow Corning and its large distributor network.

During the summer and autumn of 1973, we scheduled customer dinners in six cities across the country. Area distributors were asked to bring select key customers; OEM customers were also invited with their spouses. The highlight of each dinner was the movie that had been prepared with some of the extra money earned the previous year. It went on to win an "Industrial Oscar," and upper-level GE managers, who were invited to see what we were doing, acknowledged that it was the best product-related movie they had ever seen. To sell GE Silicone Products as a "love story" sounds ridiculous, but that is what we did. That was a real risk!

In June of that year, Jack invited Dave Dance, a GE vice chairman, to visit Waterford, perhaps because it was obvious we had the best performance of the six businesses reporting to Jack. We had put together a presentation for the visit that Jack helped us "invigorate" the day before the meeting. I was up until 3 a.m. the night before with a graphics team to prepare the changes. When Jack and Dave arrived at 9 a.m., we passed out a full-color, 20-page, hardcopy presentation that had been totally revised overnight. Jack was delighted with our effort, so going that extra mile to produce a first-class document was another big win for everyone involved.

Dave left with a trunk full of consumer silicone products that we were introducing to the general public. They probably equipped his family with enough bathtub sealant, caulk, and similar products to last them for years. More importantly, these products demonstrated we were not content to sit still on our old industrial product line, but were aggressively moving into new consumer markets with enthusiasm and commitment.

Only later would I learn why Jack had brought Dave to Waterford.

A SURPRISE PROMOTION

Knowing that Jack took the first couple of weeks in August for his vacation to go to his place on Nantucket, his direct reports took that time for our vacations as well, gambling that there would be few interruptions during that period. My wife, Anne, and our three teenage sons trailered our 24-foot sailboat to Woods Hole, Mass., and sailed to Martha's Vineyard, making sure to avoid Nantucket. Living on the boat was very cozy with each day presenting a new adventure.

During my vacation in August, I learned that Jack had just been promoted to group executive. So I was curious about who would become my new boss. Knowing that I was the least senior of his reports, I assumed it was not my turn to succeed him. In fact, I loved the job I had since I was intimately involved in every decision that had to be made in a business that concentrated on one material in a hundred different forms. And we really had only one competitor. I was learning while taking risks right and left.

Also exciting was our effort to expand beyond the U.S. At the time, we had a few distributors in South America and licenses with Bayer and British Chemical in Europe. The major expansion move was to establish a new joint venture with Toshiba Silicone in Japan. Consequently, we found ourselves in the middle of building a new silicone plant in northern Japan. I visited the site—a 50-acre rice field, reviewed the project, and learned about the marketing program for Japan. This was a new experience for me, but I felt comfortable with the plan and was eager to have it become a springboard for GE Silicone Products to really become an international business.

Upon returning to Waterford, I was very pleased, feeling that my risk-taking style had really worked in growing this business:

- We believed in our product and didn't give in on price.

- We inspired our distributors and our own people. We made business FUN!

- We entered new markets and new countries.

- We were a team working together that would not be satisfied with the *status quo*.

All of these positives were bolstered by my enthusiasm for General Electric. It was great to work for a division manager who had been promoted to group executive partly as a result of the rapid growth at my business. I could see a great future just remaining in my current position. At the end of my first year, I had received a salary increase, a substantial cash bonus, and more stock options. Moreover, unlike being in a start-up, I did not have to spend half my time raising money. Also, I reported to an experienced business manager—not 50 friends, family members, and some venture capital fund managers who would be the shareholders in a typical startup. I had employees with experience who wanted to be led, trained, and promoted in good time. I had GE experts in finance, legal, and human resources to help me. Best of all, the company had a research lab available for an occasional breakthrough, as well as providing frequent answers to tough processing questions. If some type of equipment was required for a short while, it could possibly be found elsewhere in the company. And every segment of the corporation was willing to help the others... or rue the day it was discovered they failed to cooperate.

My family and I had a great vacation. On returning to my office, I was surprised to have a message to call Jack. I assumed he wanted to tell me who would be replacing him as division general manager.

You can imagine my surprise when Jack told me that I had been selected to succeed him as head of the Chemical and Materials Division, and it had been approved right up to Dave Dance and Reg Jones. That's why Dave had recently visited Waterford. The new position would bring a nice increase in pay and bonus opportunities; it also meant I would be eligible to become a company officer. However, I had to serve a six-month probation before my name would be advanced for approval to the GE Board of Directors for confirmation as a vice president. I knew this was the custom and most candidates were confirmed shortly after the six-month period.

Then Jack said, "You know that the Chemical and Materials Division is the biggest group in the company, and Reg says it is ready to be split, but not yet.   So be aware that within a year, it will be divided in two. One will probably be the Plastics Division, and all the other departments, including Carboloy (cemented carbide tooling), Laminated Products, Insulating Materials, Specialty Materials, and Silicone Products will make up the other division. You may want to continue to live in Schenectady until this is resolved. If you should take the multi-business division, Schenectady would be a logical headquarters, with two of the businesses and the Research Laboratory being in your backyard."

This time Jack did not even ask if I wanted the job. We both knew that when a selection is important enough to require the approval of Reg Jones, if you're chosen and you want to stay with the company, your answer had better be "yes."

It was hard to believe that I had gone from heading a business in 1969, with $150,000 in sales, to being appointed head of a $500 million business in 1973. Fortunately, it did not require a family move. And though I had a 75-minute commute to division headquarters in Pittsfield, Mass., I would frequently stay overnight to lessen the wear.

Jack had already selected my replacement at Silicone Products. Don DeBacker was another chemical engineer who had a fast rise to a section-level position in the Plastics Department. Jack suggested that I announce these two changes the next morning, and Don would join me in Waterford for the rest of the week. Jack would continue managing the division until I showed up in Pittsfield the following week. Also, I learned that, unlike most group executives who moved their headquarters to Fairfield, Conn., where GE had its corporate headquarters, Jack had gotten permission from Reg Jones to keep his headquarters in Pittsfield.

It was three miles away from my new offices, but even that was too close for me. If there was any area of disappointment in this move, it was that Jack would still be the cognizant GE corporate officer for the Pittsfield area, a designation I would have enjoyed. But one can't have everything.

LESSONS LEARNED

1. An entrepreneur becoming a general manager for the first time will have many opportunities to demonstrate his/her skill. In a well-managed company, success is recognized and rewarded. Failure may be occasionally pardoned if good effort has been demonstrated. Leading change is expected, so risk-taking is normal. However, it must be approached incrementally as you prove that you can evaluate what is reasonable.

2. Coming up with your own occasional enterprising idea, be it a pricing, manufacturing, or marketing insight, is fine. Better yet is instilling the enthusiasm for everyone to think "outside the box." You may become a referee in prioritizing which projects are affordable, but you will find that the best ideas usually come from an engaged and enthusiastic staff.

3. Don't be satisfied with the *status quo*. A budget is not just a goal; it is a benchmark to surpass. Give credit even for efforts that fail (or, as Jack put it, "Reward someone for taking a swing."). Acknowledge everyone who deserves credit, but also let people know poor effort is unacceptable.

4. Make work fun. Allow occasional flexibility in scheduling if it helps someone solve a personal problem. But make sure it doesn't become a habit for an employee.

5. Don't hide bad news or exaggerate good results. Respect your suppliers, customers, and all others associated with your business. There are many other business books filled with such *bon mots*, but as a new general manager, recognize that you have hundreds of

employees, families, and customers who are counting on you not to screw up. Surprise them by doing much better than expected.

6. Just as Jack had now taken two appointment risks with me, I looked for opportunities to reward top unit managers when a section level appointment was due. Nothing is more satisfying than seeing one of your promising staff people accept a promotion and then succeed beyond expectations.

7. Lastly, a general manager sets the culture for the business. We were developing a team of entrepreneurs at Silicone Products, a process that I expected to continue even after my departure.

Chapter 8

Taking Risks Managing a Multi-Business Division

ON ARRIVING AT PITTSFIELD on the last Monday in August, 1973, I knew pretty much what to expect. Jack had taken his personal secretary across town when he relocated to new headquarters and had chosen my secretary for me, if I had no objections. Jean Tyminski knew the Plastics organization very well, and with that being half the division, she was a vital asset. From the first, we got along very well. Jean liked taking shorthand, which was important to me, and she knew how to handle confidential information.

It's amazing how few documents were in the desk: manpower folders on my direct reports, budgets and strategic plans for each of the six businesses, some corporate regulations, and phone books. Not much else. It reminded me that I was no longer intimately involved in a single business. Each of the six businesses had unique customers, manufacturing processes, suppliers, and strategies. Four of them—Carboloy, Plastics, Specialty Materials, and Silicone—were considered growth enterprises, while Laminated Products and Insulating Materials were expected to be cash producers to help fund the growing businesses.

My initial challenge would be mentoring, measuring, challenging, and overseeing the businesses. The department general managers wouldn't be very happy if I started second-guessing their decisions. With Silicone Products, I had to work extra hard to avoid getting too involved in Don DeBacker's every move. Fortunately, on things like manpower decisions, he appreciated my help. Of course, I would have to approve any of his new direct reports.

As expected, I had calls waiting from each of the six department general managers, all offering the expected congratulations and invitations to get together. I made it a point of saying that I wanted to come to their offices and visit their facilities and scheduled the following five, consecutive workdays to do just that. My headquarters was in the same building as the Plastics GM's office, so that visit was easy. Insulating Materials was based in Schenectady, Laminated Products and Specialty Materials in Ohio, and Carboloy on the outskirts of Detroit. What made the travel easy was that Jack had a turboprop airplane that would be at my disposal when he did not need it himself. It was especially helpful in making trips from and to the small Pittsfield airport.

ASSESSING THE SITUATION

My initial tour resulted in no surprises, partly because I had been at a two-day division staff meeting in June when all the strategic plans had been discussed. I also knew that Jack did not tolerate surprises, so most issues had been well resolved before he stepped up to group-level management. However, two problems remained unresolved. In Plastics, one of their proposed new products required a raw material that was only available from a chemical company that was the sole-source supplier and also intending to make the same new polymer themselves. The GM of the plastics business had not been able to convince the president of this company to release a tank car full of the required basic chemical. It was hoped that I might bring a new, friendlier face from GE to the negotiations. Jack was aware of this issue when he left; I wasn't sure I had any better chance to resolve the problem.

I argued it would actually be an advantage to both companies to have two suppliers of this new polymer, since large users, such as the automotive industry, did not like to make parts out of material only available from one supplier. That logic appealed to the company's president and the logjam was broken. I was off to a good start, though I knew Plastics needed to develop a second supplier for this chemical compound to avoid similar problems in the future.

The second issue was at Laminated Products, which had a side business making a part called Textolite© that was totally different from the normal laminate board. This side business had its own small plant in Texas and the GM of the business had filed an appropriations request for a doubling of the size of the factory. Jack had stalled making the decision to approve the AR, possibly because the department general manager was a golfing buddy. So I was given the job of assessing the request and making a decision. On our first meeting, the GM hoped that I would approve it on the spot, but, never having seen the plant or the product, I felt it was worth my while to visit the Texas facility.

Arriving there, I found a neat, productive plant, but only running two shifts per day. While sales were increasing, the market did not seem to have that much potential and it could only gain so much market share. To his profound unhappiness, I deferred approval until we had explored the possibility of a third shift and other opportunities for increasing productivity. While not denying that an expansion might be needed, I wanted to have these alternatives explored before committing the effort and capital such an expansion would entail.

When I reported this back to Jack, he was delighted that I had made the visit and was willing to wear the "black hat." So, I got hits for my first two times at bat.

Unfortunately, back in August, I had been scheduled to attend a press briefing for a new silicone sealant at Sardi's Restaurant in Manhattan. The date conflicted with the end of the corporate officers meetings at the GE Education Center, in Crotonville, N.Y., that was scheduled to end at 11:30 a.m. following CEO Reg Jones' wrap-up remarks. Don DeBacker, the Silicones GM, really wanted me to attend his event, which was to begin at 12:30 p.m. A year or so earlier, I had seen a helicopter pick up some corporate officers, perhaps even Reg Jones, on a meadow next to the Crotonville Conference Center. I knew there was a helicopter landing site on the East River, not too far from Sardi's. So I reserved a helicopter and, perhaps feeling a bit guilty for spending the money—not that it was all that expensive—decided not to mention it to Jack.

The press conference was a huge success and I was anxious to tell Jack how well it went the next morning. The moment I entered his office, I knew I was in for a scolding. Before I could say a word about the success of the product introduction, Jack furiously informed me that Reg Jones had asked him if he knew who was using the helicopter that had lifted off five minutes after his talk. By any chance had I been in that helicopter? So, I learned, again, not to give Jack any surprises. Fortunately, after a few days, it was forgotten.

MAKING A MARK

It was now November 1, 1973, and the U.S. economy, which had been growing strongly the past several years, was losing its head of steam. Yet, as each business came to Pittsfield to present their 1974 budgets, I found that the enthusiastic successes of the past were being carried over to the 1974 budget projections. My main task was instilling a sense of caution into the expectations of the GMs. We cut expenses wherever possible, resulting in a division budget compiled from the six departments that was in tune with the corporate outlook. Especially satisfying was the effort we collectively made to look for ways to decrease advertising outlays that were as much as 10% of the G & A expenses for some businesses. We hoped to make the cuts without reducing our effectiveness. Jack was delighted that we were "facing reality."

I now had the problem, however, of providing an example of reducing costs myself. A division sales and management meeting scheduled on December 5 had been planned even before Jack Welch got promoted. Now, it was my responsibility to show it could be a success without spending the money that my previous business meeting held at Vail for the Silicone Department had cost. The Plastics Department had an advertising specialist named Rich Stevens who worked directly with me at Silicone on that meeting. We initially found that in early December, snow would be better in Utah than in Colorado, and Deer Park, not far from Salt Lake City, gave us a great deal on room and board for 100 attendees. One of the company themes at that time was gender diversity and, when we looked at the list of expected attendees, there was not one woman in the group. Someone proposed we invite Nancy Dickerson, NBC business reporter and personality to be our dinner speaker. Her goal was to challenge us on what women could do for business organizations. Our choice turned out to be a big hit with the GE corporate staff. Moreover, her fee was less than half of what Jim McKay charged at Vail.

We also had a theme song that was a take-off on a hit at the time called "Bridge over Troubled Waters." With new lyrics supplied by Rich, we incorporated our budget theme to that melody, and the businesses followed up with presentations on how they were reducing costs.

The meeting was hailed as a great success and business units were helping each other. As the year drew to a close, I was gratified with my acceptance by the general managers on my team and pleased with the proposals we put forward for 1974.

In the back of my mind was the caution Jack had made about the possibility of splitting the division. While it would be a disappointment to not be heading the biggest division in the company, such a split would mean I could have my office back in Schenectady.

Being the manager of multiple businesses, yet not being a CEO, limited my opportunities to be as entrepreneurial in a personal way as I would have liked. I sympathized with the vice-chairmen and group executives of the company who were in similar positions. Though I was trying to create a culture where taking risks would be a way of life for everyone in my organization, I expected to be taking fewer myself.

Little did I know, however, what was to happen before the year was out. For an entrepreneur, life is always exciting.

CONCLUSIONS

Being a manager of multiple corporate businesses does not give an entrepreneur the same hands-on opportunities as does the position of a business general manager. On the other hand, you can concentrate on the "culture," not the details.

During my four months in this position, I nurtured the winning culture Jack was fostering. In a way, the economic slow-down in the autumn presented me with several opportunities to make changes even in well-managed businesses:

1. Even a growing business must tighten its belt when the economy slows.

2. Running a tight ship can still be fun and you will find the tools to reward your staff through modest dinners, sales meetings, and incentive programs.

3. More time is available for thinking creatively, not second-guessing your business managers, but looking for new business areas to enter through acquisition and licensing, adding diversity to your existing business operations, and discovering opportunities for amalgamating services.

4. Developing leaders is a special responsibility for which a business general manager often does not make time. This is where you can set a good example for your entire division.

5. Serving the corporation on special assignments is an opportunity for you to become better known by the executive officers. But this must never be done at the expense of managing your division.

Chapter 9

Taking Risks at GE Medical Systems

WHEN YOU WORK for an entrepreneur, you better expect surprises. For weeks, I had been wondering when Jack would split my division, the company's largest and most profitable. Jack had told me that I could choose my half of it and, within reason, choose my headquarters. People had gotten word of his promise and speculated that I would choose the five materials businesses and give up Plastics. This would allow me to stay in Schenectady, close to Silicone Products and Insulating Materials, while also being near the Research and Development Center.

I also knew if I didn't stub my toe, I was due to be elected a GE vice president in a couple of months. My biggest regret was that my dad had died the year before, and I would not be able to share with him this accomplishment.

Of course, with Jack, one never knew what to expect, so when he called me to come to his office, not far from my own in Pittsfield, it was not an unusual request.

He opened the conversation by saying that the general manager of the Medical Systems Division in Milwaukee had been unable to get that business moving forward. As a result, he was being relieved and Jack wanted me to take over that business, rather than a half of what I currently had. He told me that his Plastics and materials associates could provide candidates for the two positions that would result from the break-up into two divisions. Except for me, Jack said he had no good candidate to take on the Milwaukee challenge.

Then, he said, as I knew, having been a small part of Medical Systems only two years earlier, "This business has never made much money for GE and has never really been an integral part of the company." Jack noted that Charlier had never used the Research Lab even though Dr. William D. Coolidge had invented the first really practical x-ray tube there. "Personally," he went on, "I think GE should sell the business, but what I want you to do is go out there for no more than a year and tell me if there are any good reasons for keeping it. Don't worry, because I will have a division-level job available for you if we do sell the medical imaging business."

While I tried to catch my breath, Jack added, "Let your sons finish out their school year in Niskayuna and we will decide this summer if it is worth moving your family to Wisconsin."

I warned Jack that even though my Medical Ventures business had been in that component, I knew nothing about the x-ray imaging business and had been trained as a chemical engineer.

Jack has the knack to make people feel good about themselves and now he did his "schmoozing." "Walt," he replied, "I know you and you know me, and that is far more important than your knowledge about x-ray equipment. There is no one else in the company I would trust with this assignment. This is strictly between us, you understand."

What could I say, except to stammer, "When do you want me to start?"

"We'll fly out together this coming Monday morning (December 17, 1973). The staff there is expecting me for lunch, but they have no idea you will be with me. OK?"

That was what reporting to Jack was like—one surprise after another. But as I drove back to the office, I was really excited. There would be some advantages to this assignment for an entrepreneur:

1. I would not be following him as head of a division that he had made the fastest growing in the company.

2. I didn't let on, but I did like the idea of running the medical equipment business, perhaps inspired by keeping that poor woman alive for eight days on the MVO membrane lung.

3. Julien Charlier could have been a more congenial boss when MVO was transferred to his control in 1970. My feeling was that he had a divided team, half loving him for the leeway he gave them and half wanting stronger direction. Similar to when I returned to the silicone business, I at least knew the team, though this time they barely were acquainted with me, except as a venture manager who made no significant contribution to their profitability (but hadn't cost them anything, either).

4. The more I thought about it, the more excited I got. Once again, I would have my own business, unlike the Chemical and Materials Division where GMs ran the individual businesses on a day-to-day basis. And since Jack had handed it over to me in such good shape, there was no opportunity to imprint myself onto the organization by changing any of the business leaders. At least, Jack had credited me with a few wins, and I would be leaving with the division making its budget and well positioned for what was expected to be a tougher year for most businesses in 1974.

5. I would be the only GE senior executive in Milwaukee.

6. Lastly, Milwaukee seemed like a nice place, based on my several short trips there. And, if you like traditional German food, there is no place better for such culinary delights in the U.S.

For a few days, I couldn't say a word to anyone except my wife and secretary, both of whom had proven to me that they could be trusted with such a secret. I spent two days quietly preparing job appraisals for my direct reports, another strong tradition at GE.

A NEW CHAPTER BEGINS

Monday, December 17, was stormy from the very beginning. Jack had leased a Cessna Citation, and the trip to Milwaukee against a headwind was about as far as the plane could go without refueling. For three hours in the plane, Jack and I conversed, starting with Medical System Division's estimated financials for 1973. We reviewed the product sales, which had not been $200 million as many believed, since $80 million of the total volume had come from re-selling Kodak and DuPont x-ray film as an accommodation for the 3,000 or so autonomous x-ray departments in the U.S. Thus, there was practically no profit to GE from this business. Then there was the separate biomedical section that sold medical monitoring equipment and heart pacemakers. It generated $20 million in sales and no profit while reinvesting in a newly developing business. That left $100 million for the x-ray imaging equipment business—$20 million in service and $80 million in equipment sales. The service business was considered to be profitable. But it was hard to say for sure since replacement parts were supplied by the manufacturing section. How to price parts you transfer to the service business is always an issue.

Sales had been growing slightly, and were forecast to pick up steam in 1974. As was the case with Silicone Products, the budget for the division had already been set at $215 million.

Net income in the first half of 1973 had been $2 million, but the business had lost $1 million in the second half—totally unacceptable to Jack. The 1974 budget included a $2.5 million profit projection, but neither of us had any idea if that could be achieved. Jack had not spent much time on the business once he decided Charlier had to be replaced. The more I heard, the more risky this move felt.

We did schedule a three-day strategy review session for mid-February that would include Jack's strategist, Mike Allen, and my strategic planning manager from the Chemical and Materials Division, Al Fried. I would later ask Al to transfer from Pittsfield to Milwaukee and was fairly confident that he would be happy to come with me. There was, however, a person in Milwaukee who held that position and I would have to deal with him first. In

Jack's fashion, this strategy meeting would be held in Vail, Colo. What location could be better in the middle of February?

We were late landing in Milwaukee, but it felt good to be met at the airport by the Medical Systems chauffeur, Joe Raduka, who had been so helpful to me whenever I came out there for an infrequent staff meeting. We drove in the pouring rain to the division office on Electric Avenue near downtown Milwaukee and walked to the private dining room, where the staff had been waiting for an hour.

Upon my unexpected appearance, they quickly discerned that a new general manager was being brought in. They had assumed that the Medical Systems chief financial officer, whom they all knew well, would be named to replace Charlier. After all, he had often been used in this capacity during Jim's time away from Milwaukee, including month-long trips to Europe. The staff had become used to the CFO being in charge.

Jack did not give out any plaudits. He was unhappy they had missed their budget and the fish entrée was really bad. (I remembered to keep in mind that Jack did not care much for fish.) I hardly knew what to say, except that I would spend the next five days listening and then we would all take off Christmas week as scheduled. I would see most of them the following week at the GE Management Conference in Belleair, Fla. But I would spend all my time this week learning all I could about the business. At least, we didn't need to cancel our family Christmas vacation plans.

With that said, Jack quickly departed. I met my new secretary, who was not happy about the change (I soon brought in Rose Corey who worked with me throughout my tenure in Milwaukee), and started staff interviews, including dinners, over the next four days.

Over the year-end holiday, I summarized my initial conclusions from the staff interviews. While the order backlog for x-ray equipment was consistent with meeting the sales budget for 1974, the problem was that many of the orders were for new x-ray systems that we had never delivered before. One thing my predecessor enjoyed was designing new products, each of which was interesting. Unfortunately, manufacturing was being overwhelmed with first-time production of too many new x-ray systems at once; the shop was desperately behind schedule.

MAKING TOUGH CALLS

I hated to start off the New Year with canceling half-finished product programs, but some simply had to be delayed. For example, a few million dollars of orders were in the backlog for a neuro x-ray imager called the Omnitome. The system could turn a seated patient at any angle to help flow iodine contrast media into the ventricles of the brain before x-ray imaging. Unfortunately, both Siemens of Germany and Philips of the Netherlands, our primary competitors, had well-accepted products already in the marketplace. Ours would not be all that different. Even though the business had spent several million dollars developing this product, it had to go. The sales force was not happy.

Another problem soon came to light. We distributed a radioactive cobalt therapy system that was produced by Atomic Energy of Canada Limited. Years before, the Massachusetts General Hospital had bought one of these units from us. Now, we learned that a woman to be radiated for breast cancer had been killed when the gurney used to raise her body to the right distance below the huge lead collimator that defines the beam of high energy x-rays failed to stop at the correct height, crushed her chest between the gurney and collimator. Our investigation showed that a hospital research technician, doing some experiments on this system, had bypassed the safety switches that were specifically meant to prevent this from happening. GE was only the distributor and servicing agent for the machine, but we had the deepest pockets and were easier to sue. The claim was settled for $3.5 million.

In reviewing this with Jack, it became clear that we should not be in that business. The distribution margins were not that large and should a similar accident occur, we would again be the "deep pockets." One more blow to the order backlog.

This list of activities made good fodder for discussion at Vail as the four of us—Jack, Al Fried, Mike Allen, and I—talked about Medical Systems. I knew enough by now to explain why so many different types of x-ray systems were required and why some new products were being cut. Much of this discussion related to sales and marketing plans aimed at improving the condition of the business prior to selling it. The skiing was better than the business outlook.

After returning to Milwaukee, I looked forward to my first meeting with the 26 district sales managers who were coming in for their biennial conference. They would be joined by the four regional sales managers, plus the top sales staff. I was scheduled to address the group at dinner, but decided to attend the opening meeting that morning where the marketing manager was to introduce an important new product. We were catching up with our major competitors by announcing the introduction of an x-ray system specifically designed for imaging a woman's breast for cancer detection. This was one of the new products designed by my predecessor that had survived the elimination round. It was already in pre-production, so orders were needed.

The marketing manager gave an excellent presentation, with lots of slides, emphasizing the features of this system. I was delighted. However, the field sales managers quickly expressed their dissatisfaction that the product lacked certain new features already announced by another of our competitors at the previous December's Radiological Society of North America meeting, the traditional venue for introducing new imaging systems. The underlying complaint was that we were lagging behind with our new machine. No one had a good word to offer. My blood pressure rose, especially because the sales general manager had not interrupted this barrage of critical questioning. It was time to take a risk.

Interrupting the questioning, I went to the podium and reminded the sales managers that 12 months ago, they had had a representative, along with Service, on the new product sign-off committee. Everyone had approved this product before it was introduced to the plant. I reminded them that such a complex design could not be changed overnight without delaying the introduction of the product. At least we had a machine that would incorporate features more advanced than some competitors. We had the best service organization in the country to maintain the machine and, if the sales force were as good as it claimed to be, they should be able to get orders for the new product. Moreover, I was already looking forward to an improved model that we could introduce at the next RSNA meeting the following fall. All of their suggestions would be welcome in trying to improve the next model. I did not get a standing ovation.

At the dinner that evening, many of the field sales managers complimented me on my remarks and admitted that they deserved some criticism. They understood that I was going to be less tolerant of complainers than my predecessor had been. As it turned out, the next model was much better.

NEW THREATS, NEW OPPORTUNITIES

A week later, the marketing manager and I were sharing lunch when he said, "Oh, by the way. . .", an expression that always got my attention. What he told me was that a year before, a British company called EMI had announced a new type of x-ray head scanner that could visualize tumors in the brain in an entirely new way. It combined a computer and scanner with a pencil beam of x-rays that transversed a plane through the brain from many different directions. Though it required over four minutes to image a single "slice," it could directly visualize tumors—a huge breakthrough. And it cost twice as much as the conventional neuro x-ray system we had cancelled four weeks before (thank God for that decision). I wondered why I was not told about this device—the so-called "CAT" scanner—earlier.

As it turns out, GE had learned about the EMI scanner *three years before* when EMI had given us an opportunity to become their U.S. distributor. My predecessor, Charlier, was interested and proposed to sell 75 scanners over the first five years. EMI thought GE should sell 75 in the first year, whereupon it decided to form its own U.S. distributorship. In 1973, orders for 12 units were received, mostly in the U.S., and all from prestigious teaching hospitals. By February, 1974, the radiology community was abuzz about the results from these installed units. It was obvious that EMI could sell 75 units in a full year. Meanwhile, GE and the other traditional x-ray imaging equipment suppliers were seeing orders for some conventional x-ray units cancelled as hospitals redirected their resources toward acquiring expensive CAT scanners of their own.

I could not believe I had been there for over two months and had not heard about this technology. Both Sales and Marketing probably felt guilty about underestimating how big this market was likely to be. But keeping quiet about it was hardly the right answer.

I got more and more excited as I learned about this invention by EMI's Godfrey Hounsfield. It was the kind of technical breakthrough that most companies can only dream about. I immediately appointed a team of experts representing each segment of the business to prepare a proposal as our response. Though Marketing was represented, I put the engineering manager in charge of the committee. It seemed that almost every week, another company announced they were developing a competitive model.

After a month of intensive investigation, including a visit to the Mayo Clinic, where an EMI scanner had already been installed for nine months, the team gave me their recommendation. It was to develop a two-minute scanner, similar to what a number of x-ray companies had already announced. I was disappointed and asked what the GE Research & Development Center had recommended. When they told me the team had not visited Schenectady, I couldn't believe it. I was furious with the team and with myself for not making sure they visited the Research Lab. Though I had to admit that the Corporate R & D Center had done very little for GE Medical Systems in the previous decade, I needed a better idea than the same "me too," two-minute scanner that most competitors were already developing.

I immediately called Art Bueche and made an appointment for several of our team to visit Schenectady. The lab had just two weeks to prepare a presentation and totally surprised us by proposing to build a *five-second* CT scanner. This would mean that CT scanning would no longer be limited to the brain, but could image every part of the body except the beating heart. I was ecstatic by the promise, though aware of the huge risks involved.

The challenges were many: instead of the scanner having 12 photomultiplier-tube detectors to capture the x-rays, a five-second scanner would require 300 or more detectors just 2-millimeters in width—a fraction of the size of the smallest photomultiplier tube. Also, the computation of an image in what we called a "fan-beam scanner" required different mathematics than the EMI translate-rotate design. It had never been done before.

As we flew back to Milwaukee, my associates, while also excited about the R & D Center's idea, reminded me that it was still only an idea. Further, the Research Lab typically took years to complete a project of such magnitude. ("This five-second scanner will never allow us to become a competitive player in this market for at least five years.") They also estimated that the Milwaukee team could have a two-minute scanner ready in 18 months. I was certain EMI would already be working on substantial improvements to their product and suspected they would be delivering a vastly better, faster scanner within six months.

I called Art the next day, first to congratulate him and his team and, second, to let him know about the concerns the Milwaukee team strongly emphasized on our flight home. I reminded Art that Godfrey Hounsfield had spent seven years developing the first EMI machine and that we were estimating 18 months to develop a two-minute prototype. Could the Research Lab have a five-second prototype ready in 18 months?

Art said he heard similar comments after their presentation; before we left Schenectady, he had already assigned Rowland "Red" Redington, an experienced laboratory scientist, to direct the project. Red was putting together an 18-month project; details would soon follow. A few days later, I learned that this development effort would consist of three 6-month periods. The first was to develop a new type of x-ray detector, recognizing that 300 or more detectors, each 2-mm in width, would be required for the five-second scanner. The goal was to have a 12-detector array to demonstrate what would be needed for the full array.

Also, with the help of a consultant from the University of Buffalo, the Research Laboratory would simulate a fan-beam scanner on a computer, then take a virtual scan and, using totally new mathematics, calculate a CT image.

They estimated that, following the completion of the first set of requirements, they would then be able to build a five-inch diameter prototype in six months and, assuming its success, build a whole-body scanner in another six months. That meant that in 18 months, we could go from concept to working prototype. My team didn't believe it.

Fortunately, Art Bueche was an entrepreneur, just like me. We both appreciated the impact this proposed scanner could have on the medical imaging industry. He swore to keep the project on schedule, and I committed to not waste time and money in Milwaukee developing a two-minute scanner. I let him know that the team had discovered a start-up company working on a two-minute head scanner that we could acquire for "peanuts." But our expectation was to act only as the distributor, not become the manufacturer. Simply by learning to service this distributed product would give our field sales and service teams a huge head start in supporting our own scanner when it was ready.

Jack Welch heard of our agreement and was delighted. I told him that my budget had no extra money to cover this project at the R & D Center, except for the annual assessment we had long been paying with little benefit. So, in a way, I was claiming the previous twenty years' payments were cash advances from Medical Systems in anticipation of future benefits.

TENDING TO BUSINESS

Meanwhile, we were working hard to make our sales and profit budgets. Thanks to some new products and a real team effort, we were succeeding in meeting our financial commitments month by month. The thought of selling the business never arose again. In August, the family moved to Milwaukee.

During the fall of 1974, we met with the R & D Center staff frequently and went to Schenectady in late December for a progress report on the new detector system and the computer simulation. We knew that several routes to micro-detectors were being pursued and that the invention of a xenon gas detector was looking most promising. At the meeting, we heard that the day before, the detector team had finally gotten a 12-element detector array to work. They now knew how to progress to a 125-detector array for the five-inch prototype. The computer simulation also was successful and gave us an idea of how massive the image computer, known as a "parallel processor," would have to be. The only bad news was that rumors GE was pursuing a "fan beam scanner" had leaked to the imaging industry. Godfrey Hounsfield, the "father" of the technology, stated publicly that he had thought of this approach but had proved that it would not work. His comments worried me, but they helped us in our pursuit of a patent.

Five months into 1975, the R & D Center's progress on the five-second prototype was proceeding on schedule and was expected to yield images within the next 30 days, thus meeting the target for that part of the program. Without even waiting to see the pictures, we authorized the Lab to begin designing the full-scale, whole-body scanner. Our agreed goal was to have it ready by December 31, 1975. No one had ever pushed the Research Lab so aggressively and they thrived on it.

During the summer of 1975, I attended a joint meeting of Milwaukee engineers with scientists from the Schenectady R & D Lab. The issue was to select the three computers required for each CT scanner. Our engineers would have preferred one, perhaps two, but three seemed to be real overkill. The scientists began explaining that a huge Fourier transform (a mathematical technique to transform signals between time or space and frequency) signal would need to be created to calculate the image from all the data being collected in five seconds. Our engineers were not familiar with a Fourier transform. I could not help but recall the two weeks I spent on Fourier transforms during that special math course I took at Illinois. My acceptance helped convince the engineers to go along with their more scientific colleagues.

In July, 1975, on the basis of images from the five-inch prototype, I appointed a CT manufacturing manager and charged him with assembling a team that would temporarily move to Schenectady in October. As the full-body prototype went together, this team would start designing a production model. We would assume success like no one in the company had ever done before. We would go directly from the R & D Center prototype to production, totally bypassing an engineering prototype in Milwaukee. This approach had never been contemplated in General Electric and required teamwork between Schenectady and Milwaukee that was much closer than anything attempted before. Our engineers were being exposed to the "digital" world in record time.

Meanwhile, we were getting small cross-sectional images on the five-inch scanner from cuts of beef and even a cat cadaver. Since, at that time, the technology was generically known as the "CAT" (computerized axial tomography) scanner, I suppose it was only fitting to have a cat image. We also got permission from the FDA to test the 5-inch diameter scanner on a pendant female breast. The goals were to detect breast tumors and to differentiate between a tumor and a cyst. Eventually, this mammo scanner was shipped to Mayo Clinic for clinical testing. It was deemed interesting but not worth the extra cost as compared to conventional x-ray mammography.

ROCKING THE MARKET

Late November and the annual radiological conference in Chicago, known as RSNA, was rapidly approaching. We knew that multiple companies would be promoting their two-minute scanners and a few start-ups would be claiming to have one-minute scanners under development. By the middle of the month, we concluded that the 5-inch scanner was showing sufficient indication of what a full-scale system with 325-detectors would produce that we would announce our upcoming product at the show. Since our exhibit booth was already constructed without room for a CT display, we reserved a suite in the McCormick Place Inn adjoining the exhibition hall. Other companies had used hotel suites for customer presentations, so why not GE? Between Thanksgiving and the opening of the exhibit the following Sunday, we installed a plywood mock-up of the five-second "CT/T Scanner" (Computerized Tomography/Total Body) in the suite. On Sunday, we issued a press release announcing GE's breakthrough five-second, whole-body scanner. It was not a total surprise, but what was unexpected was that production would be starting in the spring of 1976. Our sales force was instructed to bring their best customers to the suite for a preview of the product. It was a gamble, but we were getting more confident each month. Our staff was beginning to see the benefits of taking risks.

The excitement generated by this announcement exceeded our most optimistic expectations. RSNA officials were less impressed and, at the end of the day, ordered us to close down the suite exhibit. When the motivation is high enough, you can do anything; overnight, the booth was rebuilt and the CT presentation added to our exhibit on the main floor. But the "sneak preview" in the suite gave our announcement of a 5-second scanner the impact we desired.

Of course, the radiologists were disappointed that we had no human body images to display, though we promised to have some available very soon. Our goal was to have them delay purchasing so-called "translate-rotate" scanners from the competition until our product was in production.

The Corporate R & D personnel were more excited about this project than anyone could ever recall. About eighty Research Lab employees were involved in the project, with some activities remaining in process around the clock. Between Christmas and New Year's Day, they produced the first GE body images and I saw my first whole-body, five-second images on January 2, 1976. Though they were far from perfect, we were sufficiently encouraged to take the risk of going into production.

The major problem still plaguing the technology was a so-called "ring artifact." Frankly, head images from our scanner were not as good as those from competitive four-minute scanners. The reasons weren't clear, reminding us of Dr. Hounsfield's prediction that a fan-beam scanner would never work. In spite of this difficulty, the manufacturing team now had their design completed and returned to Milwaukee where we had leased an empty grocery store as the engineering and assembly facility for the newly announced product. Further improvements in Schenectady and our expanding engineering team in Milwaukee gave me confidence that we would solve the "ring artifact" problem in good time.

In mid-February, we invited 100 of the leading radiologists in North America to the R & D Center for a series of presentations and demonstrations, including live scans of human body organs they had never seen on screen before, such as the liver. We also showed some head images, with our assurance they would be greatly improved in the production system. Fifty of these guests immediately placed deposits of $50,000 to get in line for future deliveries of our $575,000 whole-body scanner. Most already owned head scanners, which helped relieve their concerns about the "ring artifacts" in our head images.

Two months later, the prototype CT/T scanner was shipped to the radiology department of the University of California, San Francisco. This department was directed by Dr. Alexander Margulis, the preeminent academic radiology chairman in the country and highly admired around the world. His department also presented more classes on new technology to radiologists than any other medical institute anywhere. Now, with both an EMI head scanner and a GE body scanner, it was uniquely positioned to demonstrate what CT could do.

It was at this point that the R & D Center declared "victory" and reassigned the CT development team to other projects. Fortunately, several of the R & D scientists chose to move to Milwaukee to continue working on CT technology. They, along with new hires, allowed us to generate our own outstanding R & D team under Lonnie Edelheit that was making sure the technology continued to advance.

A VEXING PROBLEM

By June, the initial production model was working and became the tool for the R & D team to attack problems and develop new features. Twelve more scanners were scheduled to be produced by year end, seven of which were actually installed in hospitals before the end of December.

For the 1976 RSNA annual meeting, the CT Department, now being managed by Art Glenn, prepared a huge exhibit that included an actual production scanner. By that time, we had scores of excellent body images to display and even a few head images. But the fact remained that we really had a problem scanning the brain, though we finally understood the cause. If even one detector differed just slightly from the rest, the result was a circular streak around the image—a "ring"—corresponding to its position in the detector array. This was what Godfrey Hounsfield had predicted would be an insurmountable obstacle in the "fan beam" approach.

As we approached the show, the Milwaukee team was desperately trying to solve the problem known publicly as "rings in the brain." On Thanksgiving evening, three days before the show was to open, the engineering team was still trying to get the perfect head image. I had brought pizza to the hard-working engineers and, since they all had been exposed to test scans already, they asked if I would be willing to be the patient. I gladly climbed into the scanner and the head-holder was clamped around my skull. The scan was taken and we all waited while the computer reconstructed the time. Five minutes later, we all cheered when an image appeared on the monitor with no trace of the ring artifact. What it did have was a streak directly through the middle of the image about two pixels wide. It was caused by the clamshell head-holder not being closed completely, definitely not because my head was too big. That left a streak through the brain, ruining the image. But the important thing was the absence of rings! Since the image consisted of only 128 pixels vertically and horizontally, and with only two rows of deformed pixels, we knew it was humanly possible to manually correct the image. I asked a young engineer working on new software if he would "hand paint" these two rows to correct the image and he refused. I suppose I should have admired his integrity, but I was furious and wished I could have done it myself. Fortunately, his boss understood the situation and, by 3 a.m., had created a perfect image of my brain.

As you might have guessed, we tried another scan with the clamshell closed and got the undesirable rings we had seen before. We were close to the solution, but had not found it yet.

Nevertheless, our one good head image convinced radiologists we were on the way to a solution and the RSNA show was a great success. No one else could show anything close to the body images covering the walls of our exhibit booth. Orders poured in.

Disappointed with the reaction from the Research Lab's scientists, who felt that radiologists could "read through the ring," I told our engineering team that it was going to be up to Milwaukee to resolve this crisis.

To intensify our concern, I received a phone call from Dr. Margulis at UCSF, where the first unit had been installed and upgraded. His staff was telling him that most of their customers needed head scans; body scanning had not yet become very common. Alex said they wanted the GE unit thrown out and replaced with a two-minute EMI head scanner.

The next day, the engineering manager and I were in San Francisco to meet with the UCSF radiology staff. Alex introduced us and left the room. This was a confrontation in which he was going to be a neutral observer.

Fortunately, during December, the Milwaukee engineering team identified several things that we could try and we explained to the UCSF radiologists what we were attempting. They bought our "story" and agreed to give us six months. I believe that they were also aware that body scanning would be increasing in importance, and only the GE machine would give them the lead position in that technique.

Jack Welch was kept informed as to what was going on, of course. He learned, along with the rest of the world, that our primary competitor, Ohio Nuclear, had introduced a different type of fan-beam scanner that also had a five-second scan time and no ring problem with the head images. However, it required twice as much radiation and was considerably more expensive to manufacture than our design. Jack suggested that we should consider licensing the Ohio Nuclear design, but I felt that would have totally demoralized the GE team. Rather, we agreed to hire independent, unbiased consultants to study and compare the two designs. The intent was to have them objectively evaluate whether such a licensing strategy was the appropriate course to pursue. During the early spring, the consultants learned everything they could about the two competing designs. They concluded that the steps we were taking to eliminate the rings were promising though unproven. Like the UCSF radiology staff, they were willing to give us extra time to complete a redesign to solve the problem, but only until the end of June. If, by then, we had not eliminated the rings, then we should aggressively pursue a licensing agreement with Oho Nuclear.

For months, I felt my job was hanging in the balance. While Jack stated that he was prepared to license the technology, if necessary, I feared it would be under a different general manager.

SUCCESS AT LAST

Fortunately, both a software fix and a hardware fix combined to completely eliminate the rings. The problem that the inventor of the CT scanner, Godfrey Hounsfield, had forecast was real, but he had underestimated the ability of the GE CT team in Milwaukee. I had never been so pleased and proud of our people.

We soon announced a new model that corrected the ring problem, and also developed a retrofit for the scanners that had already been shipped. Fortunately, the hardware required for the retrofit cost only 20% of the price of the early units, while the new improved system was priced $100,000 higher than the first design. At a major strategic review that included Jack and our marketing consultants from Booz Allen, we decided to charge the early buyers, who had paid $575,000, only $100,000 to upgrade their units to what new buyers would be getting at a price of $675,000. This rewarded our early buyers by giving them the equivalent of the new model for only the incremental difference in price. Jack proposed the term "Continuum" as the marketing name for this strategy. While we did not make any profit on the retrofit, we did not lose any of our original customers, most of whom were disgruntled by the head scan issue.

To the best of our knowledge, no other imaging company had ever offered such an upgrade strategy. We used it frequently and it was eventually copied by many competitors.

In 1977, GE sold and delivered 35 new scanners and took orders for 100 more. Major competitors, such as EMI and Ohio Nuclear (renamed Technicare by then), saw their orders drop by half. We knew we had a winner, even with the problems created by the newly announced Federal "certificate of need" requirement. While competitors blamed that regulation for their loss of orders, our share of U.S. orders increased to over 50% of the total market.

GOING GLOBAL

We now believed we had a product worthy of being the flagship in a greatly expanded international effort. Our marketing studies told us that Japan had the biggest market potential of any country outside the U.S. Two years before, EMI had sold 100 CT head scanners there in a single order placed by the Japanese government. Now the radiologists had their interest whetted for a 5-second whole-body scanner.

At another strategy meeting in Milwaukee, the decision was made to have our Manager of Strategic Planning, Art Marks, head to Japan with the goal of finding a distributor who would be ready to support the sales and service effort that would be required to win in this market. We knew that the conventional x-ray market in Japan had three major players, Toshiba, Hitachi, and Shimadzu, with respective managed shares of 40, 30, and 20 percent. The remainder was imports, largely from Siemens and Philips. We did not like dealing in a "managed" market, so we looked for a distributor outside the major producers. We also knew that Siemens was discussing the importation of scanners with Toshiba, while Philips was talking to Hitachi. Our obvious partner, Shimadzu, was not that strong.

Rather, Art found a company, Yokogawa Electric Works (YEW), which was distributing a hospital monitoring system from Hewlett Packard. So they already had an electronic service and sales organization calling on hospitals. Plus their business ethics were similar to ours. So we quickly signed up YEW to sell and service GE CT scanners in Japan.

We took a huge risk by going with a company not previously involved with medical imaging, and not part of "the club." But it would prove to be perhaps the smartest move we ever made in the international marketplace.

Fairly quickly, they set up a new sub-corporation called Yokogawa Medical Systems, YMS, and soon obtained an order for the GE scanner from the prestigious Tokyo University Hospital. Though we did not yet have an export unit that would work on 50-cycle power that was not going to stop Yokogawa. They soon had a motor-generator installed on the hospital grounds to furnish

60-cycle electric current for the initial installation. Meanwhile, in Milwaukee, several 50-cycle scanners were being assembled.

Just like Alex Margulis at UCSF, the radiology chairman at Tokyo University Hospital, Prof. Akira Tasaka, was a strong leader and excellent educator. With this prestigious physician joining the GE camp, Yokogawa Medical was soon winning 40% of the orders for whole-body CT scanners in Japan. Toshiba, Hitachi, and Shimadzu must have been stunned. This success was greatly facilitated by the appointment of Al LeBlang as Executive Vice President of Yokogawa Medical Systems. Al was a long-time engineer from GE's Aerospace business and was an early member of the CT team at the GE Research Laboratory. He, along with his wife, Pat, had moved to Milwaukee in time to be involved in the initial U.S. marketing effort. With both marketing and engineering backgrounds, Al was the perfect candidate for this position. In addition, he was an excellent athlete who joined the YMS employees in golf and tennis. Also, Al was relatively short in stature, which helped make his new Japanese colleagues more comfortable in dealing with him.

GE leased an apartment for the LeBlangs within walking distance of the Imperial Hotel in Tokyo. One of Al's responsibilities was hosting multiple visits by U.S. radiologists well versed in the intricacies of the GE scanner. They would visit many of the major Japanese hospitals to make presentations on the use of the GE system. Our guests loved staying at the Imperial Hotel and being graciously entertained by the LeBlangs.

One issue that required my direct involvement was the expectation that, at some point, we would license YMS to manufacture a smaller, low-cost CT scanner specifically for the 100-bed hospitals in which most Japanese health care was delivered. Before we had reached that point, however, we discovered that Masatada Sugita, the head of YMS, had set up a "skunk works" to develop a small scanner that would be totally independent of GE. Of course, since YMS was servicing GE scanners, they knew almost all the details required to design such a system. Further, this was totally forbidden in our distribution agreement.

Mr. Sugita had to be replaced. To our delight, Shozo Yokogawa, the founder and chairman of Yokogawa Electric, appointed one of his senior executives as the new president of YMS. We soon formed a joint venture with YMS that gave the company a license and the know-how to build a small scanner. Before long, we had competitive scanners for both the major hospitals and the smaller ones as well. In addition, the latter provided an excellent product for export to third-world countries.

Germany was the next biggest market, but a very different competitive situation. Virtually every German hospital had a Siemens employee on its board and no radiologist was foolish enough to propose buying a U.S. scanner. We did look into a distribution agreement with CGR (Compagnie Générale de Radiologie), the French x-ray company owned by Thomson-Houston. They owned a huge share of the French market and had some sales in Germany and other European countries. The CGR CEO, Serge Roger, tried to convince his team that distributing GE CT products would be a successful arrangement. But that would leave their U.S. organization without a CT scanner to sell, without which they would likely soon be out of business in the U.S. On the other hand, with CGR's preferential position in the French market, it wasn't possible for GE to compete effectively there. So Europe continued to be a problem for us.

(After I had left the business to become the director of the Corporate R & D Center, Jack Welch struck a deal with Alain Gomez of Thomson S.A., CGR's parent, that traded GE's television equipment business to Thomson in exchange for CGR. I had never thought of that.)

Around this time, we learned that the Australian and New Zealand governments were going to order 15 CT scanners to add to the three EMI scanners already in Australia. All of them would come from one company to make servicing easier. We decided to move Geraldine Barry, one of the first women brought into the GE sales organization as a CT application specialist, to Sydney to pursue this contract. We had an x-ray distributor for Australia and New Zealand that had sold a few GE x-ray systems. He had an excellent technical service support capability. With his help, Geri Barry was able to win the contract for all 15 scanners—a huge order and a great inspiration for our team. We were becoming a global business.

By 1982, we had gradually grown the CT business to where we had 50% of the world market. In imaging systems overall, we now were challenging Siemens for the Number 1 position.

In the engineering organization, the effort was not reduced now that we had successful products, but actually expanded. Over the next two years, we introduced several new features in our second-generation model, called the GE CT/T 8800 that made it the gold standard in medical imaging. Eventually, the CT 9800 scanner would be announced, again with a "Continuum" option to allow 8800 customers to upgrade their equipment to the latest configuration. Today, all the remaining CT manufacturers have copied GE's "fan beam" technology. Everyone associated with the GE program has the satisfaction of knowing their efforts on this project improved millions of lives and helped make GE Medical Systems a powerhouse in the worldwide medical imaging marketplace.

During our first several years in the CT business, GE, along with all the other CT manufacturers, had been notified that we were violating EMI's patents. In our case, knowing that we would likely have to pay them a licensing fee, we began to reserve money from CT sales for that eventuality. Of course, we had filed patents from both the research at the GE Research Lab as well as from the Milwaukee research and engineering unit on the unique features of the GE fan-beam scanner. As the major imaging competitors switched over to copy our technology, we, of course, let them know that a license would be required. Licensing eventually became a bonus profit for GE.

ENTER "NMR"

While this activity in CT was driving great growth in sales and profits, a new opportunity was taking shape on the distant horizon. Two professors at the State University of New York, Raymond Damadian, M.D. and Paul Lauterbur, Ph.D., had disclosed their work on a potential new imaging technology called "nuclear magnetic resonance" (NMR). It combined a powerful magnetic field surrounding the human body and a strong radiofrequency (RF) signal. When this RF energy was "pumped" into the body, it excited the protons to release unique RF signals of their own that could be detected and used to compute an image of the body's internal structures.

NMR appeared to be so complicated that we expected it would require at least a five-year research project before it would become a competitive threat to the CT scanner business. Nevertheless, the GE R & D Center initiated a small research effort, though nothing comparable to the effort that went into the CT program. However, by 1980, we began to see images produced by an EMI scanner at Hammersmith Hospital in London. Progress was coming much faster than expected and with 50% of the world's CT orders coming to GE, our competitors were trying to steal a march on us via NMR. The greatest design variable among the different competitors was the power of the magnet used in the machine. The EMI device had a 0.1 Tesla magnet, but the various competitors were all using stronger fields in anticipation that higher field strengths would ultimately produce better images.

At the same time, EMI was still hopeful of recovering its leadership in CT imaging. The rumor had it that Dr. Hounsfield and his team were reluctantly developing a fan-beam scanner along the lines of the GE design. In their Chicago research lab, where EMI also had an imaging development laboratory, the team was determined not to emulate GE's architecture and, instead, were investigating a "nutating" design that would avoid the ring artifact problem altogether. Indeed, given time and money, this approach might have yielded good images. Unfortunately for them, the design proved expensive and mechanically complicated. EMI seemed very confused with regard to its CT developmental strategy.

I proposed to GE headquarters that EMI might be ready to consider exiting the CT business, since they were burning through cash at a prodigious rate and NMR success was still years away. Of particular interest to GE, I could see that EMI had a lead in NMR imaging research and were filing numerous patents on that technology. An acquisition of their medical business could solve GE's licensing issues in both imaging modalities.

I made a date for my boss, Ed Hood, and me to meet with the EMI chairman, Peter Laister. Though a strong champion of Godfrey Hounsfield, he was becoming disillusioned with EMI's ability to compete in the medical imaging market. Ed and I, along with the GE corporate counsel, flew to London where we met with Peter and his key aides, including his legal counsel. (Having corporate lawyers present while meeting with competitors is standard operating procedure.) While we never got down to discussing terms, Peter agreed to the concept, but noted he was having a serious problem with his vice chairman who was convinced EMI Medical could be brought back to its former prominence. Peter told us that would be his mission and we might as well enjoy a nice dinner together that night, since there was not much else to discuss until that issue was resolved.

We flew back home disappointed and weren't surprised when, two weeks later, Peter told us he would have a revolt on his hands were he to sell the medical imaging business. There was not much else for us to do.

We were to learn not long thereafter that Thorn, another British electronics giant, had acquired EMI, practically saving it from bankruptcy. Within a week, I had arranged a phone conference with the Thorn CEO; a month or so later, my new boss and I were back in London for a meeting at Thorn's headquarters. This time, we very quickly got down to terms for an acquisition of the medical device business, though we specifically excluded EMI's U.S. division because we wanted nothing to do with their "nutating" scanner. Most critically, the acquisition included licensing rights to all their CT and NMR patents. We now had a solid patent portfolio for licensing.

With that behind us, it was time to give serious thought to NMR technology. The GE R & D Center had already built 0.1 Tesla and 0.3 Tesla scanners. And we had learned that other companies using magnets of similar strength were starting to go into production. New product announcements were accompanied by better and better brain images.

To my astonishment, the Schenectady R & D Center proposed to build a product with a 2.0 Tesla magnet. Oxford Instruments, the primary supplier of superconducting magnets, had never built a body-sized magnet at that strength, but felt it was possible. Once again, the decision was up to me as to what field strength we would choose for our initial product. I took a huge risk and approved the order for a 2.0 Tesla magnet.

Nothing in this industry is secret, and the news that we were thinking about a "super high field scanner" had leaked, as tends to happen in research laboratories. Physicists with our competitors quickly told doctors that GE had overlooked a major problem that didn't affect magnets up to 0.3 Tesla. The issue was that the required frequency of the RF energy pumped into the human body increases linearly with the magnetic field, while absorption of these waves was also known to increase with higher RF frequencies. This suggested the RF signal returning from the body in a 2.0 Tesla magnet would be too weak for creating good images. However, Dr. Rowland "Red" Redington, known for his smart decisions on CT scanning and the leader of this program as well, promised to solve this problem as our program moved ahead.

"Going for the gold" had been key to our success in CT scanning, so I decided to stick with the super high-field plan. Our engineers and sales people were also now with me. The CT experience had taught everyone a valuable lesson: don't be satisfied with a "me too" approach. By 1982, a 2.0 Tesla scanner was on its way from Oxford, England, to Schenectady. As it turned out, it could only ramp up to 1.5 Tesla, but we decided not to wait for another magnet to be built. Rather, we announced to the world that GE scientists believed 1.5 Tesla was the optimum field for imaging and, further, a high field scanner would be able to do unique measurements such as spectroscopy. Our CT success provided the credibility to make some bold claims. Unlike seven years earlier, we never considered selling a machine with lesser capability. If that meant losing a year of sales to multiple competitors, so be it.

RAMPING UP THE PROGRAM

In a relatively short time, our first NMR head image was obtained and it was absolutely the best cross-sectional brain image that had ever been seen. Tumors were more visible than they were in a CT image and with no exposure to radiation or injected contrast material. On the other hand, the scanning procedure took an hour per examination, compared to minutes for a full CT procedure. Since the NMR system was twice as costly as CT, it was expected its sales penetration rate would be slow. However, since bone does not show up in NMR images, there was good reason to believe that hospitals would want both machines. Interestingly, radiologists concluded that the word "nuclear" was an unnecessary provocation and, after 1982, the technique was always called magnetic resonance imaging (MRI).

In 1981, GE sold 275 CT scanners and budgeted 300 sales for 1982, a very modest increase. January arrived with a thud when CT orders dropped nearly to zero. By March, we had taken only 25 orders; our competitors were in similar straits. We anticipated that the excitement over MRI at RSNA would have an impact on CT scanner orders, but we had no idea it would be that severe. Jack Welch had heard from some radiologist that CT devices were finished and he now predicted the death of the CT business. We had a very acrimonious meeting at GE's Fairfield (Conn.) headquarters in March at which he told us to terminate all CT development efforts and consider using the CT factory to assemble MRI machines. Obviously, we had no proof whether he was right or wrong, though our sales force was telling us there were many hospitals still operating old EMI machines that needed a five-second CT scanner. I was convinced that CT sales would rebound, but probably at a lower rate than earlier.

This was the toughest meeting I ever had with Jack. And had Ed Hood, the GE vice chairman who was also at the meeting, agreed with Jack, I was prepared to resign. Fortunately, Ed agreed with me that waiting to see what happened in the second quarter would be appropriate. I'll always be indebted to him for not panicking. It was a risk.

By the second quarter, CT orders were turning up. Though we did not make the CT sales budget for the entire year, receiving only 250 new orders in 1982, we did begin to achieve budgeted CT sales by the third quarter. With MRI orders also starting to come in, things were looking much better. And, while the CT development effort was reduced, it definitely did not go to zero.

Today, the ratio of orders for CT and MRI scanners is around one to one. That is because both are important for different diagnoses; in some cases, a diagnosis benefits from both images.

To exploit this new opportunity, GE built a totally new MRI manufacturing and engineering facility on its campus near Milwaukee. Soon, our high-field Signa™ MR system had gained the #1 position in the new MRI market, mirroring the success of GE CT scanners five years earlier. Once again, by taking the more entrepreneurial approach, we set the "Gold Standard" in medical imaging. That remains the case today, 30 years after the introduction of the GE MRI design.

Incidentally, a few years after we got our 1.5 Tesla magnet, one of our competitors, hoping to leapfrog GE, received a 2.0 Tesla magnet from Oxford Instruments. They, too, found it worked better if they lowered the field to 1.5 Tesla. Today, everyone has added a 3.0 Tesla model to their catalog, which is marginally better in its performance for some examinations. But, without question, our 1.5 Tesla system remains the "gold standard."

MANAGEMENT CHALLENGES

In 1983, our net income budget was $57 million and we felt confident we could meet that figure. Unfortunately, the group to which GE Medical Systems was assigned included two electronic businesses that were badly missing their budgets. Like us, GE Aircraft Engines was also having a good year, so when our group executive, Jim Baker, asked Brian Rowe and me to sell anything we possibly could to help him make his budget, we were happy to oblige, but feared the impact it would have on the next year's sales. I rallied our team and we actually made $64 million in profit, 12% over budget. In order to do that, we pulled forward $60 million in sales from what would have been the following year's backlog. Like a fool, I still accepted a 1984 profit budget of $67 million and was criticized for a very modest 5% increase. In fact, except for the special effort, we probably would have made a profit of $59 million in 1983, turning the $67 million budgeted for 1984 into a very favorable 15% gain.

In any event, we missed the 1984 budget by $2 million, making $65 million in profit. In 20 years, I had never missed a profit budget, so this really hurt. But I learned an important lesson: don't let an unusually high result in one year be forgotten when planning the next year's budget.

By the middle of 1985, with the CT business gradually improving and the MRI business, while still smaller than CT, growing significantly, life was good. Then, one Friday afternoon, I received a call from Jack. He said that Jim Burke, the CEO of Johnson & Johnson, the huge health care products company, had asked the two of us to meet with him in his Waldorf-Astoria suite in New York City the following Monday afternoon. Naturally, Jack asked what I thought would be the subject of such a meeting. I replied that the imaging business that J & J had acquired, Diasonics, was costing him $100 million a year and he likely wanted to sell it to us. Jack asked me to get our team cranking over the weekend and have an estimate of what Diasonics might be worth at his Manhattan office an hour before the scheduled appointment with Burke. GE does not waste time when opportunities appear.

Diasonics (earlier known as Technicare) was the company that gave GE so much grief over the "ring artifacts" in our early CT images. They had solved that problem, but with a scanner that exposed patients to more radiation and produced less detailed images. Compared to GE, they had the second largest installed base of scanners in U.S., so every one of their sites represented a potential sales opportunity for a GE scanner. We estimated Diasonics would be worth as much as $100 million to us in terms of this increased market opportunity. In addition, they had some good sales people we would be interested in bringing onto the GE team.

With this background information, Jack and I went to Jim Burke's suite. For half an hour, we heard why it had made good sense for J & J to acquire Diasonics about eight years earlier, and why it now made good sense for them to sell it. They preferred a U.S. buyer and wanted $50 million for the business. That amount just happened to be the value of the service parts that Diasonics had in inventory.

Jack and I caucused in the adjoining bedroom and could finally smile. We returned to the conference table and accepted the proposal, adding the stipulation that any inventory not used during the next year would be returned to J & J for reimbursement at full value. That was acceptable to J & J and, within four days, the company lawyers from both sides had all the documents prepared for signing. Three weeks later, Diasonics was formally transferred to GE ownership. Employee severance payments were the responsibility of J & J. While it was costly, they eliminated a $100 million annual loss going forward. It was a win-win deal for both companies. (By the way, we sold very little of their replacement parts inventory, giving us a big refund some time later.)

In 1986, we further grew our international coverage by forming a joint venture in South Korea with Samsung. Like Yokogawa in Japan, Samsung had a small medical instrument business, but had no CT or MRI products. The Korean market wasn't large, but the joint venture with GE soon made Samsung Medical Systems the number one imaging supplier there.

In China, the government totally controlled purchasing of expensive medical equipment; a woman radiologist affiliated with the Peoples Liberation Army was in charge of major equipment purchases. They wanted our scanner, but also wanted our expertise in making simple x-ray equipment. We agreed to help their army factory make a low-cost, mobile x-ray imager, giving GE an important advantage in their subsequent CT and MRI purchases. Soon, our Asian partners produced, to our design, lower-cost scanners that would be affordable to the smaller hospitals and clinics outside the U.S. At very little cost, we were able to provide an array of scanners ranging in price from $200,000 to $2 million.

MORE CUSTOMER VALUE

Our product sales were always profitable, but we learned to earn supplemental income in several ways.

First of all, many hospitals preferred to lease their GE CT and MRI scanners. We made an agreement with GE Capital that effectively allowed them to purchase the scanners from us at the price negotiated with the customers. Then we would share with them the interest income made during the course of the five-year lease. Secondly, we would offer customers a five-year equipment service contract that assured maintenance expenses would never exceed a predictable amount they could budget. Third, since the average life of a CT scanner x-ray tube was around 20,000 scans, we would give customers a prorated credit toward a replacement should their tube fail earlier, similar to the replacement warranty on an automobile battery.

The CT tube warranty was popular. Users learned that if they did not run the tube at too high a current, they could win by stretching its life. And even if they were aggressive and the tube failed early, GE took the hit. Things were in balance until we introduced an improved, faster CT scanner. Suddenly, these great stresses were causing many tubes to fail after just 5,000 or so slices and it was all we could do to make replacement tubes fast enough. Simultaneously, we launched a program to research the problem and work to increase tube performance. During those dark days, we modified the pricing of x-ray tubes to $1 a slice, no matter how few slices it actually performed. In the minds of customers, this move turned x-ray tubes into a simple consumable item and bought us time to develop a solution. Thanks to the great efforts of the tube team, led by Jerry Cote, we soon had average tube life back up to 20,000 slices and, eventually, 100,000 slices. Shipping a tube felt to us like shipping a Porsche.

Equipment accessories were another valuable source of incremental revenue, such as improved MRI head-holders and similar devices that would be developed over the lifetime of a system. Improved software was another profitable enterprise. If the customer purchased a warranty package, they would receive software enhancements at no additional charge. Otherwise, they could buy the software for a fee. Since software represented a zero cost in materials to us, we began to understand why Microsoft was so profitable.

Jack loved how we were making quality and leadership so profitable. We just had to make sure that we also were helping our customers to also be profitable. We worked very hard on customer relations.

We also took an entrepreneurial approach to RSNA where all the exhibitors would lavishly entertain radiologists, administrators, and their spouses. Whether as a reward for past sales or an enticement for future orders, this was a traditional hospitality feature of this key marketing event.

Our idea was to institute a Tuesday night gala during the RSNA week. The first was held in the ballroom at the Ritz Carlton Hotel, the finest ballroom in Chicago, for several hundred radiology chairs and their guests. It was a black-tie dinner and dance with outstanding cocktails, food, and ambience. Between courses, we showed a light-hearted film touting GE imaging systems. Most years, we would present a well-known singer, such as Jack Jones or Edie Adams, as the after-dinner entertainment. For four years, GE's RSNA gala was the hottest ticket in town. But even after we extended it to two, consecutive evenings, we couldn't accommodate the demand for tickets. Eventually we chose to end the event, rather than alienate disappointed customers and prospects. All good things must come to an end.

By the mid-1980s, ultrasound imaging was becoming a more significant factor in the imaging market. We tried to purchase one of the innovative start-up firms that was leading in this technology at the time, but they were convinced that they could do better as an independent ultrasound equipment supplier. We did acquire what was available, a true start-up with only a prototype to show. Though it never earned GE a significant position in ultrasound, at least it launched us into this new imaging segment. Perhaps the Research Lab would come up with another breakthrough technology.

In the nuclear medicine field, the gamma camera company we acquired in Denmark, to replace our previous Israeli supplier, gave us a competitive product, just not the market leadership position we had hoped to have. At least it made a quality product and allowed us to offer a complete line of imaging equipment. That was important since there were many hospitals and clinics that only would buy GE equipment.

By 1984, we were competing for the number one position all around the world with the exception of Europe. While we did well in Spain and England, where we had factories, the rest of the continent was pretty much controlled by Siemens, Philips, and CGR. In spite of that, we could tell Jack that we were number one globally in overall imaging.

ON THE ROAD AGAIN

By this time I had become vice chairman of the Milwaukee Symphony Orchestra Board of Directors and decided that a symphony tour might help us in getting better known among the radiology chairs in Europe. For $100,000—another risk—GE paid the air transportation for the orchestra to and from Europe. Lukas Foss, the music director, was an extremely well-known conductor, composer, and pianist who knew Europe well. He scheduled the orchestra in seven major cities from England to Germany. Revenue from the concerts themselves covered the orchestra's living expenses in Europe.

The musicians could not believe the enthusiastic reception they received in each city. While Milwaukeeans might give them an occasional standing ovation, the orchestra received sustained applause and multiple standing ovations from the very knowledgeable European audiences. Their rendition of Brahm's Symphony No. 1 closed each performance, which would then be followed by a private GE dinner near the concert hall for our guests and in-country sales specialists. To Maestro Foss' credit, he came to each of these seven dinners to praise GE for making the MSO's first European tour possible. I had some of my most exciting meetings ever with customers and potential customers at these events. While it didn't make us number one in Europe, the orchestral tour introduced us to many new prospects in a memorable way.

By December, 1985, I had been with the medical business for 12 years. The work was not that tiring, but going to dinners with customers made for extra-long days. Meanwhile, I had also gotten involved with Wisconsin politics and was even thinking of running for a state office. I had risen to the position of nominal treasurer for the state Republican Party organization and was involved in a Senate campaign for Bob Kasten. He ran against the incumbent, Democratic Senator Gaylord Nelson, who had represented the state for 18 years. The election eve party turned out to be a very exciting occasion. The 15-minute updated tallies started out with Bob trailing, but by 1:30 a.m., he had pulled ahead for good. What a sweet victory.

It wasn't hard to imagine myself in Bob's place, enjoying the excitement, suspense, and ultimate joy of a successful campaign.

Yes, GE was terrific, but I could see that the growth in imaging equipment sales was slowing. Therefore, much of our attention now was being spent on cost-reduction initiatives to maintain profit growth even in a slowing market environment.

This kind of effort is important work, but for an entrepreneur, it was in no way as exciting as the previous 12 years had been. So I began planning to terminate my GE career at the end of the year in order to enter into active campaigning for elective state office. Several friends had given me checks—one for $1,000— to encourage me to become involved in the Republican Party's efforts to gain the governorship.

CHANGE OF PLANS

But, once again, while I was on a holiday, this time on July 4 at Lake George, N.Y., Jack called from Nantucket to suggest what he thought would be a new, exciting opportunity for me. At the same time, it would allow him to appoint a new group executive for GE Medical Systems who was an experienced expert in cost reductions.

The position he had in mind was for me to return to Schenectady as Senior Vice President and Director of Corporate Research and Development. That also meant I would be in charge of the R & D Center.

Roland Schmitt, who had followed Art Bueche as director of the center, had been very helpful in supporting the MRI research program that had given us the "gold standard" in the industry. Roland, like me, was now looking for a less demanding position.

I thought back to my days as a first-level manager at the R & D Center and my conviction that an engineer could never become the laboratory director. I would be the first to test whether an engineer can direct research efforts. It also meant Anne and I would be getting back East, nearer our three sons, now settled in the Boston area, and our cottage on Lake George. There was a lot to attract me to the idea of moving back to Schenectady.

The position also meant that I would become GE's Chief Technology Officer (CTO) and would sit on Jack's side of the table when all the top business executives came to Fairfield for their strategic and budget reviews. That sounded like a job that would give me all the challenges I wanted.

I also recognized that Jack wanted to see more business partnerships evolve with the R&D Center, such as Medical Systems had perfected through the CT and MRI development projects. My experiences would help broker similar joint programs between the center and other company businesses, perhaps leading to a new generation of breakthroughs in various GE product lines.

I could have opened negotiations and even hired a lawyer to get a better financial contract with GE, but that was not my style. Indeed, I had been very well satisfied with the financial rewards, especially the stock options, which I had received. So, without hesitation, I agreed that this opportunity was even more exciting than entering the Wisconsin political arena. One disappointment was that I would not become the board chairman of the Milwaukee Symphony Orchestra, but I knew that the board had other good candidates. Besides, I could go back and join the board of the Schenectady Symphony Orchestra whose budget was about 1% of the MSO's.

And so ended my nearly 13-year career in the medical imaging business. It had been an unbelievable success considering where the business had gone since almost being placed on the chopping block back in 1973. Along the way, imaging equipment sales and service had grown from $100 million to $2 billion, and annual profits from zero to $80 million.

Jack and I agreed that the announcement of the change would be made in both Milwaukee and Schenectady later in July. I would start my new job in Schenectady following the August vacation period. That would give Anne and me sufficient time to plan our move. Once again, I began updating manpower reviews on my staff.

ON BEING AN ENTREPRENEURIAL GENERAL MANAGER

1. As was the case when I led Silicone Products, GE Medical Systems was an ideal spot for an entrepreneur looking for challenges. In a way, I was the CEO of an "independent" company. But by being part of a large corporation, I was not saddled with so many of the functions of a stand-alone company CEO, such as raising investment money, working with a board of directors, and meeting with shareholders. I did have a boss. In fact, during my years in Milwaukee, I reported to four different GE senior vice presidents and vice chairmen. In each case, these leaders had demonstrated that they could successfully run GE businesses, so they understood my assignment and appreciated the risks I was taking. They were of considerably more help to me than most independent boards of directors are to their CEOs.

2. I found the most important rule to follow is "Keep your boss informed." If there is bad news, tell him or her immediately and ask for help. Never end a conversation without reaching a clear agreement on the plan to be executed. Listen very carefully to his or her words and, if in person, the expression on their face. Be aware that you can press your boss to back off or change his mind only a limited number of times.

3. Once in awhile, your experience in a given area may be much greater than your boss's. You may find it necessary to take a stand and say, "I'm sorry, but if we cannot reach some sort of reconciliation, please accept my resignation right now." I was fortunate the few times I needed to say that, the response was something like "If you feel that strongly about it, I guess I can wait until we get more data."

4. In a multi-business company, get to know the other business general managers and the nature of their operations. Look for ways to help each other, whether in sales, R & D, manufacturing, repositioning people to better jobs, and so forth. Determine where you may

have customers or suppliers in common. Let them know when you are interested in visiting one of their locations.

5. Get acquainted with all the corporate function managers—legal, HR, finance, manufacturing, and so on. Meet with them to see if they have any concerns with your own function managers. Are they pleased with your legal, accounting, manufacturing, and engineering staffs? Are there any ways you can help them or they help you? Keep in mind that in a crisis, they can be of tremendous assistance if your own function managers are overwhelmed.

6. Is your engineering/R&D manager making full use of the corporation's central research laboratory? Is he or she going there for occasional meetings? Does the lab send a liaison for reciprocal visits? Does that liaison occasionally stop by to see you? Should you invite that liaison to some of your strategic planning meetings?

7. Don't meddle with or nitpick your direct reports. If they are not doing their jobs, replace them. If they ask you for help, bend over backwards to either lend a hand or get them the assistance they need.

8. Review the conclusions at the end of the section on my time as general manager of Silicone Products (Chapter 7). All those points apply to any organization, whether a small department or a large division.

9. Finally, think about the culture of your business. Your people must understand the objectives of the business and be heartily committed to them. Discuss it with your HR manager and your staff. Are you all supporting the desired behavior? Remember that you set the example. If you are not having fun and enjoying your job, either change something or get out. It is that vital.

Chapter 10

Taking Risks as a Chief Technology Officer

UNLIKE MY TWO MORE RECENT MOVES, when I appeared on an August day in 1986 at the R & D Center in my new role as the Laboratory Director, my predecessor, Roland Schmitt, was still there. However, his corner office was vacant and he now was ensconced in a new office far down the hall, working as a consultant to Jack on some special projects. Taking his secretary with him, I found my secretary from 20 years before at MVO, Arlene McElroy, was available. It was comfortable to be working with her again.

Roland suspected this would not last too long, but we both knew that having him present in the Laboratory might be a problem, especially since I was expecting to take a more aggressive stance on many issues than he had been inclined to do. For example, he recognized that people would likely appeal to him about projects that I would be terminating and promised he would not interfere. Happily for us both, that agreement worked out very well; Roland's presence actually proved very helpful to me.

After six months or so of consulting, Roland became President of Rensselaer Polytechnic Institute across the Hudson River in Troy, N.Y. This was the perfect job for him.

Meanwhile, I was becoming familiar with all the R & D Center projects not connected with GE Medical Systems. These involved about 90% of the 450 Ph.D. scientists and 300 associates that made up the technical staff. A lot of new technology had been developed since I had left the lab in 1965. (I also made sure to avoid the appearance of favoring Milwaukee projects.)

EARLY IMPACT

Early on, one area that I saw as an opportunity for cost reduction and improved productivity was to reverse a decision that was made in 1966, when the GE Engineering Laboratory and the Research Laboratory were merged to form the R & D Center. The people in the Engineering Laboratory continued to work in a building at the so-called GE Main Plant about six miles away in downtown Schenectady. I maintained an office in each location and many services, such as a cafeteria and a glass shop, were duplicated at both sites. I asked my facility manager to develop a plan and estimate the cost for moving the people from the Main Plant to the Research Center. I made a point of mentioning that a significant number of scientists who had to have their own bench laboratories 20 years ago, today were working with computers and software that took up a fraction of the space. Further, the work for the machine shop and glass shop was diminishing as the trend to software development proceeded. I was hoping that the cost for this move would not be that high.

After a month of study, he reported there was no way such a consolidation could be accomplished without adding a $5 million building. That convinced me he was more interested in having a new building project than in saving money. He was so set on his approach, I concluded he wouldn't be an effective facilities manager for me. He found a new job outside the company and I hired a facilities manager from the Major Appliance business, in Louisville, Ky., who was used to operating under tight financial constraints. In six weeks, he had a plan ready for implementation that paid for itself within six months from the savings generated by the consolidation. The benefits were enormous: we could all use the same cafeteria, an important aspect of any research laboratory; we did not need a shuttle between the two sites; no one needed two offices; and duplicative technical resources were minimized. I was pleased how easy it was to have an early, positive impact as the research director. Finding the right facilities manager made all the difference.

During that site consolidation, I was also faced with an issue that arose from GE's purchase of the RCA Corporation about a year before my arrival. Jack wanted RCA, primarily, to acquire NBC, the broadcasting network. Ever since he had met Jim McKay, who spoke at my Silicone Products sales meeting in Vail many years before, Jack had the desire to own a communications company. He had tried to acquire Cox Broadcasting in 1977. But NBC was a much bigger plum, with the "Today Show," "Tonight Show," "Saturday Night Live," and many other popular prime time and news programming ratings leaders. In addition, RCA also had consumer television and aerospace businesses that would complement and strengthen GE's own activities in each of these areas.

Along with them came RCA's central research laboratory located near Princeton, N.J. It was managed by Jim Tietjen, a Ph.D. scientist who was 10 years younger than me but with a similar background. His laboratory had 1,200 employees, was costing GE $150 million a year in operating expenses, and had not instituted a contract system with the businesses as the R & D Lab had done. Clearly, GE was not prepared to support it long-term.

My predecessor at the Research Lab had informed Tietjen that GE would like to close the RCA laboratory and transfer the top 20% of their senior scientists to Schenectady to retain their experience and expertise. It would probably cost $200 million to close the Princeton lab and Jim feared that his top scientists would prefer to stay in New Jersey. After all, Bell Laboratories was not very far away.

From the first, Jim suggested that the Batelle Laboratory, in Columbus, Ohio, might be interested in acquiring the RCA Research Lab. Batelle's business was doing contract consulting work for a variety of companies in many industries, and they might see the opportunity to cover the costs of operating the RCA Lab by having its knowledge supplement research areas where Batelle was weak. As I pointed out to Jim, if there were former RCA scientists who could help GE, we would award Batelle consulting contracts to gain access to this expertise. Consequently, their skills would still be available as needed, but at a lower cost.

Jim had already approached Batelle and we jointly met with them again. After a month, however, they declined, which we had expected based on the atmosphere of our discussions. Jim then suggested the Stanford Research Institute might be a potential buyer and I took over the negotiations with Bill Miller, the CEO of the Institute. The result was that GE gave the RCA Lab to SRI, along with a five-year commitment to help fund the integration of the organizations. Obviously, if there were RCA scientists who could help GE, we would get their consulting gratis. In discounted dollars, this solution cost GE $200 million, but avoided the negative publicity and professional ill will a closure and massive layoff would have entailed. Not surprisingly, GE required little help from the former RCA researchers.

As a measure of success, several years after the transfer was completed, Jim Tietjen became the CEO of the Stanford Research Institute—a win for all thanks to our entrepreneurial solution.

AN UNEXPECTED REVOLT

In the spring of 1987, the GE Corporate Officers Meeting was held at the Arizona Biltmore Resort in Phoenix. The agenda for the meeting was for each of the 12 strategic business units (SBUs) and the corporate functions to outline current actions and future plans to cut expenses. These proposals would be even better if they could be employed in other SBUs. I related the story of consolidating the two laboratory sites in Schenectady and cutting the RCA lab as my current actions. I did not really have a good example of future plans except to terminate "hobby" projects that had been allowed to continue too long. However, I preferred to report on that after it was completed rather than expose internal Research Lab issues to the SBU managers. After all, they were being charged annual assessments of about $10 million each to support our activities. That was a fabulous deal for Medical Systems, but most of the businesses questioned if they were getting their money's worth.

I was not prepared for the strong negative attitude expressed by several of the SBU managers, especially those from GE Capital and NBC, both of whom had legitimate gripes.

At least with GE Capital, we had a software development program underway to increase productivity of telephone operators discussing mortgages with prospective homeowners. The operators needed a reliable and responsive method of accurately pricing mortgage interest rates anywhere in the country. Our expectation was that once this was perfected, both operator productivity and risks assessment skills would improve, increasing the profit to GE Capital. There could be other "smart systems" that the Laboratory could program once this initial project was proven successful.

We also were working on the development of remote TV cameras for NBC that could be aimed from the control room, thus eliminating the need for an operator on every camera. We were also developing a method to show on TV the roll of a golf ball on the putting green and, thus, forecast the optimum path to the hole. I am not sure that Bob Wright, President of NBC, even knew about these programs, but had to admit that their value might not be worth the millions NBC was being assessed.

The conclusion of that day's session was that GE would have an external assessment made of the value of the Research Laboratory to the corporation. Jack selected Booz Allen to conduct the study.

Shortly thereafter, as I was discussing this problem with GE Vice Chairman Ed Hood, to whom I officially reported, I acknowledged the legitimacy of the issue and suggested a way to find a solution acceptable to everyone. My proposal was to invite the CTOs from each of the major businesses to the R & D Center for as long as a week to thrash this out. We would kick it off when the results of the Booz Allen study were available; Ed might even keynote the meeting to underscore the importance of our undertaking. Then the attendees would simply go into "deep immersion" planning. Ed approved and the meeting was soon on the calendars of CTOs across the company.

With the group finally gathered in Schenectady, I began the session by presenting a financial history of the R & D Center's expenses and revenue sources. Some 60% of our budget was provided by the assessments levied on the 12 SBUs at a level approximately proportional to their individual operating expenses. Another

30% came from GE Corporate and, while reducing the company's earnings, did not directly affect the incomes of the various businesses. The remaining 10% came from government contracts.

My strategic partner, Marv Garfinkel, then reviewed the list of the major projects presently underway. He acknowledged that perhaps one-quarter of our activities were connected to research projects not yet ready for presentation to potentially interested businesses. I followed up by discussing our efforts to reduce costs by eliminating "hobby shops" and other initiatives, such as the site consolidation project.

Against this background, I then asked the participants from the operating units to assess the positives and negatives in our mutual partnership. For most of the businesses, their complaints really boiled down to one key point: they felt they did not have enough control over the work we professed to be doing on their behalf. That was emphatically not the case with Medical Systems and Aircraft Engines where we enjoyed true partnerships. But they were the exceptions.

The evening of the first day, Marv and I fine-tuned the proposal we were going to present. At 8 a.m. the next day, I reviewed it with Jack and Ed to make sure they were on board. Intentionally, I had not yet reviewed this proposal with my staff, assuming they would consider it had no chance of being accepted or workable—too big a risk. Welch and Hood had both approved, and that was enough for me to take a risk that the R&D staff would go along, if the businesses' engineering managers agreed.

A NEW RELATIONSHIP

The proposal was that in early September of each year, the R & D Center would make presentations to the individual businesses detailing programs we believed were far enough advanced to justify their picking up the development costs. There would be defined goals for the coming year and, while developers cannot guarantee schedules with perfect certainty, they would only be committed to support the project one year at a time. Each additional year meant they risked a possible modification or even cancellation if the Lab failed to meet expectations. Though this proposal would not change the total assessment provided by the businesses, it would divide it more fairly according to what projects each business requested that we undertook on their behalf.

In addition, we could increase the outside contract grants to 15% of our total revenues, but these contracts would need approval from one of the businesses. Another 25% of our funding would come from GE Corporate, generated by the overall assessment that the businesses were accustomed to contributing. That money would fund exploratory projects aimed at developing new programs to sell to the businesses in future years.

To make this effective, we had to know more about the strategy and needs of each business. To accomplish that, we needed to upgrade our liaisons with the businesses in the following way: instead of having a senior scientist as a liaison, we would assign a laboratory or section manager to each business. Our idea was that this liaison would be accepted by the business to the extent that he or she would be welcomed to their staff meetings. For example, the head of the Chemistry Laboratory would be the liaison to the Plastics business and was expected that he would spend up to half his time on this part of his job.

After fine-tuning, we went through an analysis of our proposal for projects with each business, keeping in mind they would be refined as budgets were being prepared for the coming year. I gave each business the opportunity to renegotiate regarding the laboratory leader we had assigned as their liaison. Since I had not yet gotten the laboratory managers' acceptances of their new responsibilities, there was still the possibility of a different liaison being proposed.

After three days, though business participants had come prepared for a five-day session, we had reached an agreement and they all returned home to tell their colleagues what had been negotiated. With Welch and Hood already having approved this plan, I felt reasonably comfortable that the businesses would agree to it as well.

Only then did Marv and I tell the Research Lab staff what had been decided. Since they were aware of the threat to close or split up the Laboratory, which they uniformly opposed, they were pleased to learn we had a chance to maintain our corporate status. However, they were seriously concerned that the businesses would not support enough of the projects that we had suggested for the next year. I was pleased that all the managers assigned to business liaison positions accepted their challenges; the former liaison scientists were moved back to their research positions.

What I was counting on was that, in the business' preliminary budgets for the next year, they had included an assessment for the R & D Center based on old regulations. I knew that when the final budget would be reviewed at Fairfield, Jack or Ed would ask each business what projects they were funding at the Research Laboratory. Since this money was already in the preliminary budget, they would more or less be expected to come close to that amount with programs they agreed to fund. They couldn't claim the money was not in their planning.

MORE COMPLAINTS RESOLVED

For two months, the Research lab staff was on tenterhooks, but by the end of the year, we had achieved the 60% funding level from the businesses on well-defined projects. At least for a couple of years, no one raised any objections about the funding methods for the Research & Development Center. Our proposal saved the laboratory.

However, businesses are always looking for ways to cut expenses. The newest threat was from a few of the business units who wanted our research effort but felt our scientists cost too much. The cost per scientist, they claimed, was much higher than it would cost if he were in the engineering function at the individual business. The gist of their complaint was that our overhead rate on a scientist's salary was about 120%; in the businesses, the rate for an engineer was only 60%.

Fortunately, my time as a business leader served me well in this argument. I was aware that in a business the total cost of an engineering department or section would not include many expenses that would be assigned to other functions of the business. For example, the engineering manager's salary would be assigned to the "administration" line in the total expense roll-up of the business. Expenses relating to finance, accounting, human relations, health care, legal, and strategic planning would all be charged to those departments in the business, not to the engineering budget. Also, most facilities costs would be charged to manufacturing. In comparison, at the Research Laboratory, all costs would be applied to the salaries of the scientists, resulting in the much higher overhead expense.

Ed Hood had learned of this latest complaint and of my rationale. He immediately called the corporate audit manager and suggested this would be an excellent project for two young auditors. In a period of three months, they did such a study and proved two things: first, on average, I was right; and, second, among the different businesses there were some with actual overhead rates of over 75%. I suspect those engineering managers wished they had never brought up the subject.

As a result of these resolved issues, we achieved a much better integration between the Research Lab and the business units on at least 90% of the projects. There were always a few projects that simply did not go as expected, whether due to problems with the research and development program, or simply because of poor market research by the business. But in every situation, the communications and feelings of a true partnership were better than ever before.

Now, with most of the disagreements between the businesses and the Research Laboratory resolved, my job became measurably easier, though there always was some issue requiring my attention. The next was within the laboratory itself where senior scientists were concerned we weren't doing enough pure research that might lead to breakthroughs of value to the businesses. While everyone in any laboratory is more or less expected to be thinking ahead and doing "bootleg research" on their new ideas, our scientists wanted more authorized funding for this type of work.

Marv and I decided to commit up to 10% of the laboratory budget to such speculative projects that were too wild to mention to a business. We asked all the scientists to submit new research ideas and announced that the best 15 proposals would be funded for up to three years. Only 30 research proposals were received. My staff individually prioritized them and then collectively selected the 15 to receive the promised research funding.

As in many research labs, there was a "Coolidge Fellowship" group made up of about 30 senior scientists, with two being added each year. It was a great honor to be selected as a "Coolidge Fellow." The reward was having a 6-12 month sabbatical, all expenses paid, to any laboratory or university that would provide an interesting learning experience. It had made some real differences in several careers.

The Coolidge Fellows, at their next quarterly meeting, voted to disapprove our method of selecting the winning research projects. In response, I suggested that the Coolidge Fellows and their staffs do their own prioritizations of the submissions during the next cycle. Though I made no absolute promises, I was hopeful of finding a middle ground between their rankings and ours.

As I expected, the rank order of the two groups was practically identical. The Fellows also learned that the selection process was more time-consuming than they had expected. With this new appreciation for the validity of the process, the Fellows were willing to let the staff make the selections without their help. That was an easy problem to solve.

ABOVE THE CLOUDS. . .

Another part of my job as GE's Chief Technology Officer was to take on special assignments, usually as the result of an issue that arose during a periodic business review held in the boardroom at corporation headquarters in Fairfield. For example, in 1988, Brian Rowe, Vice President & General Manager, Aircraft Engine Division, presented Jack and his staff with a challenge to fund a new engine for a proposed Boeing aircraft. This would be a costly endeavor, but also a huge opportunity, Brian claimed. The plane, destined to become the Boeing 777, would be the largest twin-engine passenger plane Boeing had ever made. Boeing wanted the three major jet engine manufacturers—GE, United Technologies, and Rolls Royce—to begin development of an 80,000-pound thrust (lbf) engine. This would be adequate for their present design, but it might have to grow to 100,000 lbf over the next five years to power an extended-range version of the 777, which already was being discussed with the airlines. GE's CF-56 engine had become the most popular commercial engine available, but it had been surpassed in thrust a few years back by both Rolls Royce and Pratt & Whitney designs that each produced 70,000 lbf. Naturally, they were trying to win big shares of future Boeing 777 orders for themselves.

Brian had been able to push the performance of the CF-56 from 56,000 to 72,000 lbf. However, his engineering team emphatically cautioned about significant risks in pushing the engine toward 80,000 lbf and near certain disaster if they attempted to reach the 100,000-lbf threshold. Instead, Brian proposed that GE Aircraft Engines initiate a $3 billion program to develop the proposed CF-80 engine, a new design with the potential to grow to 105,000 lbf and, perhaps, beyond.

Jack was not convinced the CF-56 couldn't be stretched to 80,000 lbf. Besides, there was no guarantee that the Boeing 777 was going to be successful enough to warrant an engine larger than 80,000 lbf.

Jack hated big expenses that weren't in the long range plan. He looked at me for the R & D Center's opinion, and I had to admit that Brian's proposal had hit me out of the blue as it had him. In order to avoid making a decision at that moment, Jack asked me to put together a team of our top research scientists to learn how the CF-56 engine might be improved. I was to report back in one month.

As had happened so often in my career, I was unexpectedly thrust into a new area of technology. That was just what I loved and what made my work so satisfying. I quickly assembled my R & D Center team and headed to Evendale, Ohio, to meet with the Aircraft Engine experts. We soon were convinced that though the technical risks of further stretching the CF-56 design were acceptable, fuel consumption would be significantly higher than in the proposed CF-80 design. For airline customers, engine operating costs in the era of high and rising petroleum prices trumped most other considerations. Thus, we saw no alternative but to make this $3 billion investment.

By the time we reported this to Jack, he had reconciled himself to going forward with the project. And the Lab's combustion experts and I were a lot smarter about the workings of a GE engine. As it turned out, the GE90, as it was called, was a huge success.

. . .TO THE HOME KITCHEN

On another occasion, the Major Appliances business in Louisville had introduced a new compressor for its latest consumer refrigerator. It was less noisy and required less power than its predecessor. During the first year after its introduction, production and sales of refrigerators using that compressor amounted to well over one million units.

About nine months after the shipments began, the service organization began receiving complaints from customers about noisy refrigerators that would not keep the ice cream frozen. Replacing the compressor corrected the problem, but the cost of the serviceman's time and a replacement compressor was several times more than the profit we were making on that refrigerator. It was not unusual for a new product to require some extra service for awhile, but usually a fix is found that can be implemented in the production process and, in some cases, even retrofitted to installed units to avoid future problems. In this instance, however, an analysis of the failed compressors revealed unusual wear in a rotating bearing that had not been encountered before.

The head of engineering at Major Appliances proposed to solve this problem with a totally different compressor design that would put less pressure on the surface of this bearing. Our metallurgist at the Research Lab believed that a new metal alloy used in this new bearing was causing the problem and recommended going back to earlier materials with slight modifications. The biggest problem was that it took a couple of months of accelerated testing to reach a detectable-wear level, during which time the failure was growing to the point where field failures would soon equal the production of new compressors. Jack was counting on us to recommend where the main effort should go. We concluded that trying to solve the problem with a new, unproved mechanical design was a greater risk than going back to the earlier bearing material. Fortunately, the previous material worked fine and the problem was consequently solved in a relatively short while, though at a cost of tens of millions of dollars in warranty expenses. This was one more area in which I needed to become expert in a new technology.

I was beginning to see that this type of consulting might present an opportunity for me after retirement from General Electric. I was approaching 65, which is the required time of retirement for GE senior executives. From the time I had joined the Research Lab, Jack and I had discussed at the annual manpower reviews who might be my successor. At one of these sessions, I mentioned that my CT scanner engineering manager some 10 years earlier, Lonnie Edelheit, had the potential to take on such a position. He had left GE about five years previously and was CEO of a small medical ultrasound company in Seattle. I knew he enjoyed living in the Northwest, but had heard a rumor that his company was about to be acquired by Siemens.

Jack also knew Lonnie and, in his usual fashion, wasted no time in getting Lonnie on the telephone. Within 15 minutes, he had convinced Lonnie to come to Fairfield for an interview and, a month later, the two of them negotiated a contract that would have Lonnie become a new laboratory manager reporting to me in Schenectady. There would be a golden parachute for him if he did not ultimately become my replacement. Over the next year, he met our expectations and so, in September, 1992, I announced my retirement at the end of the year. For four months, we worked together to prepare the budget and operation plans for 1993. He became the seventh director of GE's R & D Center on January 1, 1993.

There was no part of my long career that was more relaxing than these final few months. I was gratified to see that GE Medical Systems had continued to hold the number one world share in medical imaging. With new improvements coming from research and development, both in Milwaukee and Schenectady, GE CT and MRI systems remained the gold standards among radiologists around the world.

Going into 1990, the R & D Center produced the first digital ultrasound imaging system ever built. It had so many circuit boards that it was at least four times as big as conventional ultrasound systems of that era. But we knew integrated circuits were increasing in capability and decreasing in size at an amazing pace. This prototype allowed GE to learn what added benefits digitalization could provide in image quality over the previous analog ultrasound designs.

Today, all new ultrasound systems are digital. In a unit the size of a laptop computer, a doctor can now produce the same, if not better images, than were gotten with the one-ton original prototype. There is even an advanced GE ultrasound device, hardly larger than a cell phone, that physicians can take with them on their daily patient rounds.

Following in the footsteps of such giants as Willis Whitney, Charles Steinmetz, William D. Coolidge, and Guy Suits in leading the famous GE R & D Center was the most satisfying conclusion to my corporate career I could have ever imagined. My hope was that what I had learned would prove equally useful to the start-up companies where I planned to invest my future time, talent, and resources.

CONCLUSIONS

During the last two decades of the 20th century, many corporate research centers were disbanded, usually because their associated businesses did not feel they had received appropriate value. This could easily have happened at General Electric as well, but by working with the engineering managers of the businesses, we found a solution to this criticism while leaving the research center with sufficient resources and funding to continue developing significant breakthroughs that meet the needs of most GE businesses.

In my case, the fact that I had been both a scientist and a research manager at the R & D Center early in my career and then had gone on to direct GE company businesses for 20 years before returning to run the laboratory, gave me the practical experience and credibility to resolve the problems that cripple most central research laboratories.

Being away from research for 25 year may also have been a benefit. So much had happened in technology during that time that I knew my own scientific knowledge was outmoded and incomplete compared to that of the current crop of the scientists, young and old alike.

This meant I was not inclined to be inventing things or trying to outguess the experts. I could ask questions, however, and especially appreciated scientists who could explain their work in terms that the engineers in a business could understand. Perhaps I was helped in this by being a chemical engineer, rather than a pure research scientist. In fact, my experience in directing the Research Lab proved successful enough that of my immediate successors, two were engineers and one a physicist.

It also helps for a laboratory director to explore new ways to encourage scientists in different technologies to communicate with their peers in other specialties. To accomplish this, I ensured that there was only one cafeteria in the laboratory complex to facilitate the sharing of lunch—and ideas. I also found that encouraging social organizations, such as sports teams and even an employee glee club open to everyone in the organization, helped reinforce camaraderie. Sponsoring a social hour after work on Friday afternoons, including beer and wine, turned out to be effective in breaking down the walls between departments. I found that many of the same friendship-enhancing events customary in a business, such as employee family picnics, worked very well in the laboratory culture as well.

I also found it valuable to question predictions of how long a given research project might take. For instance, if a unit manager told me it would take one year, I would ask why it couldn't be completed in nine months. Many times, I found they really had no firm basis for their estimation and that a shorter time frame was perfectly achievable. On the other hand, if you gave them a year, it would certainly take that long.

Whenever senior scientists complained that we in management did not know what we were doing, I would try to give them the leeway to do the task as they thought right. If they had a good plan of action and a successful outcome, then it was a win-win for everyone. But if the project turned out to be more difficult than anticipated, then they usually were willing to follow management's proposals the next time.

Most important of all, a research director should be willing to take risks and encourage others to do the same. But a truly entrepreneurial director will not allow a central laboratory to become a collection of "hobby shops."

Chapter 11

Observing Jack Welch as a Leader and Risk-taker

IN PREVIOUS CHAPTERS, I talked about my personal experiences and entrepreneurial opportunities as a CTO for a large corporation and as the president or general manager of specific businesses. This chapter is about the entrepreneurial activities of a CEO in charge of a multi-business corporation.

My personal experience with CEOs was working for Jack Welch, the legendary leader of General Electric during the last two decades of the last century. I was instrumental in bringing him into the company 30 years before my retirement and basically reported to him for the last 20 of those years. Under him were 12 remarkably varied businesses, one of which, GE Plastics, was his route to becoming a multi-business manager. But by the time he became GE chairman and CEO, his attention to that enterprise was no more intense than to any of the other businesses in the corporation. As you will see, Jack demonstrated that even as a CEO he could still be an excellent entrepreneur himself. To his great credit, he also encouraged risk-taking in all the businesses under him.

There are many books, by Jack and others, I recommend to those interested in a detailed, in-depth examination of his career and accomplishments. My objective here is to concentrate on areas and occasions where "taking risks" helped make him an exceptional CEO. I know of no other individual leader who had as much impact on a large corporation as did Jack during the 30-plus years I was able to observe him from close range. His risk-taking, I believe, is the reason *Fortune* selected him as the "CEO of the 20th Century."

AN IMPATIENCE TO WIN

From that day back in 1960, when the professors at the University of Illinois recommended to me that GE strongly consider Jack Welch for employment, it was obvious that he was an entrepreneur. He wasn't interested in the slow pace of upward growth typical for most research laboratory positions, but let it be known, right from the beginning, that he wanted to be part of a business. A polymer start-up proved to be the ideal match for his aspirations. Immediately upon joining GE, he demonstrated a most aggressive and entrepreneurial mindset, growing his PPO business faster than the company had ever seen a materials business reach commercialization. He built an $8 million "semi-works" to prove the production process and also to make product for sale. When the first applications for the product did not work out, he was willing to take the risk of completely changing the material. The new product, totally a different plastic but still containing PPO as a critical component, soon found its role in the marketplace; his Noryl™ project quickly became a success.

Before long, Jack was in charge of the entire plastics business, by which time he saw the poly-carbonate polymer, called Lexan™, as the major engine for future growth. As he described in his own book, *Straight from the Gut*, Jack set out to create a new market for the material, especially in the automotive industry. Along the way, he also totally changed the culture of the plastics business. First, he hired the popular comedy duo, "Bob and Ray," and flooded the Detroit morning radio shows with their Lexan-sponsored comic routines especially tailored to all the tens of thousands of people associated with the local automakers. He followed up by building an application center at the business' headquarters in Pittsfield, Mass., then duplicated that center in Detroit, the Netherlands, and Japan. Risk-taking, pure and simple.

To demonstrate the indestructibility of Lexan, he had a TV commercial produced showing a "bull in the china shop." The plastic industry had never seen the like of these advertisements. Of course, he did not personally produce them, but he hired the marketing talent that could convert his ideas into award-winning advertisements. His sales people loved him because he made their jobs easy. He developed an *esprit de corps* among the sales personnel that resulted in many wins and many winners. A number of his employees went on to earn general management positions in the company.

Jack knew he had a product for the world, not just the United States. Most companies would have exported Lexan to Europe; Jack built a plant in the Netherlands. In Japan, he formed a joint venture with a Japanese company that assumed the cost burden of building a production plant there. During the 10 years Jack was involved with GE Plastics, sales ballooned from $50 million to $400 million. When he was appointed Vice President and General Manager of the Chemical and Materials Division in 1971, he became the youngest corporate officer in GE history.

Shortly after he took this position, Jack appointed me to head up Silicone Products, beginning a close business association that would continue until my retirement two decades later. (Chapter 7 recounts my experiences as a new general manager in one of the smaller departments in Jack's division and how Silicone's extraordinary results helped both of us become recognized as winners.)

CULTURAL REVOLUTION

As Jack began to explore the total range of products in the Chemical and Materials Division, he made entrepreneurial moves right and left, selling one department, allowing another to reduce its budgeted income in order to be more aggressive in the marketplace, setting up new product divisions, and terminating others. And all this time, he was pushing all the businesses to be aggressive overseas—that is, if they wished to remain a part of General Electric.

Knowing there were potential synergies among GE's six materials businesses, Jack scheduled meetings where their managers could get to know each other and explore new ways to cooperate. Though there were few opportunities from a technical perspective to combine products, there were opportunities to move people from one business to another. GE Plastics was an especially rich source of sales and marketing experts for the other businesses, while Silicone Products contributed several manufacturing leaders. Several R&D managers also moved from one business to another. In two years, Jack changed the culture of the entire materials business, earning it a reputation as the most entrepreneurial place in the company to work.

Though Jack had been a company officer for just two years, he was promoted to Senior Vice President and Group Executive of the Components and Materials Group. A few months later, I became the general manager of the Plastics and Materials Division and eligible to become a company vice president. Once again, I was in a good position to observe how Jack applied his unique style of leadership to four diverse business divisions: Plastics and Materials, Electrical Components, Appliance Components, and Medical Systems.

When Jack soon found he could not relate well to the vice president at Medical Systems, he offered the man a severance package he could not refuse. After an extremely short stay at the Plastics and Materials Division, I found myself directing the Medical Systems Division, as discussed in a previous chapter.

With me running Medical Systems, having been well-trained under him by this time, and another friend and reliable colleague in charge of Plastics and Materials, Jack was able to direct the bulk of his attention to the other two divisions. He soon determined neither of them was ever going to be a growth business, What they did provide was an excellent opportunity to show senior company management that he knew not only how to lead growth businesses but how to "harvest" businesses as well. He soon had these two divisions generating more cash for the company than had ever been expected.

It was about this time when Reg Jones, GE's chairman, and his vice chairmen were beginning the winnowing process to select Reg's successor. Twelve potential candidates were identified and most given the top positions in totally different businesses in order to demonstrate their versatility. Jack was moved to the leadership of the Consumer Group, one of the 12 strategic business units in the company at that time. I saw very little of him over the next two years as he worked to turn around the challenging Major Appliances business. I could see that he did not find the entrepreneurial opportunities there as enticing as he had hoped they would be. However, his group also included GE Capital where he saw great opportunities for rapid, profitable growth. In short order, GE Capital was becoming the fasting growing unit the company had ever seen.

ULTIMATE LEADERSHIP

Two years after that appointment, Jack was named the new CEO and, in 1981, at just 43 years of age, he became the head of one of the largest corporations in the world. Shortly afterwards, my reporting was shifted to Vice Chairman Ed Hood, one of two who reported to Jack. Ed had spent his entire career in the Aircraft Engine business, which still reported to him. He loved that business and had modest interest in Medical Systems. So, on request, I addressed my monthly reports to both Ed and Jack. Jack loved Medical Systems for what it had done for his career. Not surprisingly, I got many more written comments on my reports and telephone calls from Jack than from Ed. Both Ed and I understood the reasons.

One might be excused for supposing that Jack would lose some of his entrepreneurial energy now that he had achieved the position he had aimed for from the day he joined GE. That absolutely was not the case. Few large, multi-business corporations have ever been managed by such a brilliant entrepreneur as Jack Welch. So let me comment here on what an "insider" observed of the entrepreneurial moves that a strong CEO can implement even in a very successful, century-old company.

1. AT HIS FIRST OPPORTUNITY, Jack looked at the environment of the Corporate Management Meeting, an annual, five-day "kick-off" session each January involving up to 500 GE managers. For decades it had always occurred in the first week after New Year's and always at the grand old hotel near Clearwater, Fla., called the Belleview Biltmore. It was a 100-year-old wooden colossus with hundreds of big guest rooms, but such a potential firetrap that the company hired guards to walk the halls at night looking and smelling for smoke. The golf course was good, but not great, as was the food.

Jack immediately moved the conference to the Boca Raton Resort on the Atlantic coast with modern rooms and conference facilities, a great improvement over the Biltmore. The meeting began with a Sunday evening cocktail party and ended promptly after Wednesday lunch, not dragging on until Friday noon. Later, Jack took one more step, suggesting that individual businesses have their own meetings on those newly available days, possibly in Boca Raton, but not necessarily. By the end of these sessions, over 2,000 GE managers had received Jack's message, along with the input from company stars and outside speakers chosen by Jack to both inspire and challenge us.

Individual presentations had to be very well prepared, with lots of visuals to make them serious, interesting, and useful to multiple businesses. Jack's final speech on Wednesday was really hard-hitting, starkly painting our challenges for the year ahead, but still sending us away feeling like a conquering army. Everyone understood GE was a first-class company with prospects second to none.

2. NEXT, JACK ESTABLISHED a Corporate Officers Council that would meet for a day-and-a-half two or three weeks before the end of each quarter. This took place at corporate headquarters in Fairfield and there was no golf—it was all business. Attendees included the twelve SBU presidents, plus six senior corporate officers representing the various functions of the corporation.

A typical session would begin with GE's chief financial officer, Dennis Dammerman, giving us a simple tabulation of the expected earnings per share for each of the twelve SBUs, based upon the projections we each had supplied. He would then add up the numbers to arrive at an earnings per share target—$1.05, for example. Jack would then take over and let us know that the investment analysts were estimating that GE were going to make, say, a $1.10 a share, and we weren't going to leave until we had figured out how to do it.

Jack would then start at the top and, for instance, remind Aircraft Engines that they had been boasting how their jet engines were requiring less repair work than ever before. Yet, Jack would point out, Brian Rowe, the SBU president, had not reduced his warranty reserve. Jack would suggest a modest reduction was justified that would add another one cent per share for the stockholders.

When Medical Systems' turn came, Jack would know to the penny that if we sold four more MRIs before the end of the quarter, we could add a half-cent to the earnings per share. If we had to give product warranty for an extra year to get the scanner accepted a week earlier, it was worth it. So he would go down the list in that fashion, knowing where there were opportunities that all of us could achieve, if necessary. It may sound a little like a game, but it worked. During my decade of attending these meetings, we never missed the analysts' estimates. And each SBU felt it was being equally "stretched," which was very important.

Once the financial package was put to bed, each SBU would give a report on its business situation. If there were items that might be helpful to other businesses, it would generate extra attention. These reports had to be realistic and accurate; it was not a good idea to hide problems. Besides, by the time you finished your presentation, oftentimes there might be several solutions offered. These were really good learning sessions for business leaders.

There also was time for the top legal officer to discuss new regulations; the human resources senior vice president to discuss personnel issues; the R&D senior vice president to report on major projects; and so forth. These sessions were never boring and we felt like a team, with Jack our coach and captain.

3. PRIOR TO JACK BECOMING CEO, each SBU prepared and forwarded to headquarters an annual "strategic plan" book perhaps 200 pages in length. There were a number of strategic planning specialists in Fairfield who would dissect these books looking for errors—"gotchas"—as they tried to second guess the businesses. Jack duplicated what he had done as a division manager, requiring each business to present no more than 12 pages of information. These plans would be reviewed by the CEO, the vice chairmen, and the staff senior vice presidents in a two-to-three hour review in the boardroom. Each SBU manager would bring key staff members and they would sit on one side of the table, facing Jack and his staff on the other.

From the first page of the book, this would be a two-way conversation with Jack contributing most of the questions and ideas, usually directed at the SBU manager, but sometimes at staff vice presidents if Jack thought they should be involved. As CTO, I would also be questioned by Jack, who expected me to already be very familiar with each SBU's technical issues.

These sessions occurred once a year in March, but out of them came many changes in the businesses, especially with regard to overseas operations, major capital expenditures, introduction of new products, acquisitions and divestitures, and so on. Jack would come to the meeting very familiar with each of the previous year's plans, including his annotations. Business was really pretty simple and with few surprises the way Jack practiced it.

4. JACK ALSO HAD A DIFFERENT APPROACH to budgeting. As with the strategic plan, budget presentations were based on a relatively few number of pages (though, of course, they were backed up by scores of pages created by the SBU finance staffs). The real meat was in the discussions with Jack and his senior staff in October of each year. Where Jack differed from other CEOs was in differentiating a budget required for financial planning from a budget based on searching for opportunities. For example, for 100 years, GE managers had budgeted to improve working capital turnover by 1-2% each year. That was still what the financial managers felt comfortable with. Jack did not want to waste a minute on incremental performance. The question you had to be prepared for was, "How can you reduce working capital, inventory, or receivables by 10–20%, or even 50%? Think outside the box, then tell me why that won't work." In my time reporting to Jack, I saw working capital "turns" double, creating hundreds of millions of dollars in cash for the company.

"If the normal cycle to develop a new product is three years, how can it be cut in half?" was another of his frequent queries. His questions ranged widely, from whether we should be licensing patents, buying a start-up, or taking the risk of using our own research to leapfrog the competition.

Of course, many of these ideas required investment and/or risks, and they could not all be funded. But at least they were open to consideration. It was also an opportunity for Jack to check if a SBU was aware of what the competition was doing and what customers were saying about GE products. Were doctors asking for a new device from the Medical Systems business, or were we trying to push it onto them?

Budgeting wasn't just about money; it was really about ideas. And at the end of this effort, each business would be prepared to write a much better budget document than it had going into the corporate review.

5. JACK HAS OFTEN SAID he spent as much as 70% of his time on personnel development. Much has been written about his requiring "totem-poling" of employees, but the way it was handled at General Electric was never as rigid as many critics supposed. No one ever learned that they were in the bottom 10% of employees and about to be fired without being given a year to escape from that unwanted category. Most people who were forced to leave GE realized that they were better off taking a position where they could be at least an average employee, as compared to being an employee continually in the bottom half.

On the other end of the scale, Jack created great incentives for improvement, especially when he increased the percent of employees receiving GE stock options. Being in the top 10% was almost a guarantee of stock options, a wonderful incentive in a fast-growing, entrepreneurial corporation. In later years, many employees thanked me for the options they received, saying they had put their kids through college with the proceeds.

Another area where Jack took an entrepreneurial approach was in selecting leaders on their management potential, as much as on their technical or sales expertise. Recognizing that all businesses had different challenges and opportunities, Jack tended to appoint managers who could best manage in that situation, rather than based on their experience in a specific business function. For example, the general manager of a "cash cow" business would have different skills than the general manager of a fast-growing, short-cycle business.

6. FROM THE VERY BEGINNING, Jack appreciated that a CEO could only expect to be successful in pushing one "thrust" at a time. Whether it was "transparency," "business effectiveness," "Work-out," "best practices," "globalization," "Six Sigma," or "digitalization," he relished the satisfaction that came when they succeeded. Each thrust lasted about two years, after which it had become embedded in the company's culture. Using his entrepreneurial approach, he was a master at selling these concepts. Books have been written on each of these thrusts, but what is important is that over the 20 years that Jack was a CEO, GE sales grew from $27 billion to $110 billion, earnings grew from $1.65 billion to $10 billion, and the stock value from $13 billion to $334 billion. That would not have happened without Jack convincing everyone that these thrusts were for real.

7. IN STAFF FUNCTIONS, Jack also was an entrepreneur. He built an outstanding "inside" legal staff, which greatly reduced the need and expense for outside legal counsel. He brought in creative speechwriters and new staff managers for the critical areas of investor and public relations. He reduced tenfold the Corporate Strategic Planning staff. His primary corporate objective was in steering the twelve SBUs to maximize return to the stockholders with their unique strategies. The corporation was the sum of these efforts. Jack provided the vision.

As an operating general manager, it was wonderful not having a corporate planner second-guessing me. I could work well within the vision.

These are examples of a single CEO's entrepreneurial efforts. What must be added to this list is Jack's encouragement for all of his employees, but, especially, his business general managers, to also be entrepreneurs. . . to take risks. Failure could occasionally be tolerated and even rewarded, though not frequently. "Winning through failure" was not his strategy. Incremental tactics would not be accepted long-term.

Similarly, the U.S. will not prevail by just cutting costs and taking the same route that other countries are pursuing. When American corporations are entrepreneurial and willing to take risks, no foreign competitor can match us.

Afterword

I HOPE I HAVE INSPIRED YOU to be always on the attack, looking for opportunities to take the risk required to create change, perhaps even produce a breakthrough. I have found this is the best recipe for making a job the most enjoyable.

Mutually supported by teammates with that same spirit, I found it was possible to accomplish results that filled all of us with professional and personal satisfaction. Thus, I was able to retire from GE with the conviction that my colleagues and I had helped make the world a better place.

In my 42 years at GE, I had a few bad days. On returning home, Anne would always know. Though they were few in number, I couldn't imagine having to live through them without having each other for consolation. We also are blessed to have raised three wonderful sons, taking some risks along the way there as well. I am pleased that they and their families are also risk-takers in their own unique ways.

If we had it all to do over again, I think there is very little Anne and I would change.

Acknowledgements

IN THIS BOOK, I HAVE TRIED along the way to identify and thank the many people that molded my life and career. From my parents to Jack Welch, there were folks that let me take risks and, in so doing, allowed me to have enormous fun and accomplish a few dreams. Only in America—from Abe Lincoln to Jack Welch, folks from modest origins have evolved into leaders of significant stature. Where else could that happen?

My own beginnings were neither as modest, nor were my accomplishments as great. But, one step at a time, people gave me opportunities and challenges that I grabbed as eagerly as gold. What I made out of these opportunities, I always felt I owed to everyone who bestowed them on me. But I was rarely alone. Especially at GE, I was always part of a team. We worked toward common goals and I thank everyone, many still living and others now passed on, who worked with me. Our teamwork accomplished so much. Thank you all for going along with my risks.

On today's team, my office manager since GE retirement 20 years ago has been Jim Lohre. We met in Milwaukee, where he refined my personal investment proficiency. Then Jim and his wife, Karen, came to Schenectady where he became my Man Friday as we opened my technical consultancy business, Vantage Management. Among his many talents, Jim can type as fast as

I speak, and most of this book was dictated to him. But he has been more than my stenographer. He edited and rewrote text that needed clarification or embellishment. Beyond that, he kept me going when I needed a push. Jim, this book would never have been written without you.

On the publishing side, I went back to the team that published *Envision: A History of the GE Healthcare Business 1893 – 2008* by Leon Janssen and Gene Medford (2009 Meadow Brook Farm Publishing LLC). They have added a professional touch to my amateur ramblings.

An early, critical reviewer of my book was a member of the GE Board of Directors whom I got to know because he was the liaison to the GE R & D Center. Dr. Frank Rhodes, now the President Emeritus of Cornell University, read and marked so many grammatical mistakes in an early draft that I was embarrassed. Frank, I hope you find this version a more polished effort.

Acknowledgements are usually directed to friends who helped with the book, but, since this is likely to be my only such effort, I must also take this opportunity to recognize and thank my family who aided me in all my efforts. First I want to acknowledge my parents, Ruth and George Robb; my siblings Kay and Herb; and, for more years than you can count, my wife Anne for encouraging my risk-taking. Then thanks to our three sons, Rich, Steve and Lindsey; our daughters-in-law, Marge and Kim; and, finally, our five granddaughters, Mackenzie, Kelsey, Hayley, Carly, and Kyle, for bringing Anne and me so much joy. We are "family" in the best of ways: they have supported and made it possible for me to take professional risks without having to worry about family concerns.

Jack Welch recently thanked Anne for putting up with me and my travels. He was right "on the button." Now, as I end this literary effort, Anne and I are celebrating our 60th Wedding Anniversary. We have been truly blessed.

About Walt Robb

DR. WALTER L. ROBB is currently a management consultant and President of Vantage Management, Inc., in Latham, N.Y. He retired from General Electric Company in 1993 following a 42-year career in a variety of technical, management, and executive roles. He capped his long career serving for seven years as GE's Senior Vice President for Corporate Research and Development, and as the company's Chief Technology Officer and member of the Corporate Executive Council. In that position, he directed the Schenectady, N.Y.-based General Electric Research and Development Center, one of the world's oldest industrial laboratories. And with some 1,650 employees—including more than 1,000 scientists, engineers, and technicians representing virtually every major scientific and engineering discipline—one of the largest and most diversified.

Prior to assuming his corporate R&D role, Dr. Robb was Senior Vice President and General Manager of GE Medical Systems, headquartered in Milwaukee, Wis. Over a period of 13 years, he led that organization's growth from a $100 million supplier of medical x-ray gear into the world's leading producer of high-technology medical diagnostic imaging equipment with $2 billion in annual sales. Under his management, GE introduced "fan beam" computed tomography and "high field" magnetic resonance technologies that continue to serve as the "gold standards" in medical imaging. In addition, his foresight also helped establish GE Medical Systems as a leader in ultrasound and nuclear medicine as well.

Dr Robb joined General Electric Company in 1951, first serving as a chemical engineer at the Knolls Atomic Power Laboratory in Schenectady, where he performed research on nuclear fuel reprocessing and isotope separation. In 1956, he transferred to the GE Research Laboratory (later a part of the Research and Development Center) where he developed advanced membranes. In 1962, he became Manager of the Center's Chemical Process branch.

As a result of this experience, Dr. Robb was awarded 12 patents primarily dealing with permeable membranes and separation processes, and is the author of more than a score of papers published in various professional journals. His research earned him six I-R 100 Awards, sponsored by *Industrial Research* magazine, for "the most significant new technical innovations of the year." His work on artificial gills and immobilized-liquid membranes gained him international recognition, including coverage in *Life* magazine.

Dr. Robb was appointed Manager of Research and Development at GE's Silicone Products Department, Waterford, N.Y., in 1966; Manager of the GE Medical Ventures Operation in 1968; and General Manager, Silicone Products Department, in 1971. He took over as General Manager of GE Medical Systems in 1973 and was elected a General Electric vice president the following year. In 1983, he was named Senior Vice President and Group Executive when the business was elevated to a GE "group."

Dr. Robb is a member of the National Academy of Engineering. In 1989, he became the first recipient of the Medical Technology Leadership Award presented by the Diagnostic Imaging and Therapy Systems Division of the National Electrical Manufacturers Association. He holds honorary doctor of engineering degrees from Worcester Polytechnic Institute (1988) and the Milwaukee School of Engineering (1994). In 1987, he was presented The Pennsylvania State University Distinguished Alumni Award. He received the National Medal of Technology from President

Clinton, in September, 1993, for his leadership in the CT and MR imaging industry.

Following his GE retirement, Dr. Robb has served on the Penn State Leonhard Center Advisory Council, and on the Engineering Advancement Council at Johns Hopkins University. He was on the Scientific Advisory Board at the Morgridge Institute for Research at the University of Wisconsin-Madison, and on the Industrial Advancement Council at Lawrence Livermore National Laboratory. He is Director and Treasurer of the Double H Ranch for sick children in the Adirondack Mountains, and a board member of Union Graduate College where he also co-teaches a course on leadership. He is a former Senior Elder for his church in Schenectady.

In the business arena, Dr. Robb was on the boards of directors of Celgene Corp. and Cree, Inc. during their formation years. Presently, he is on the board of Mechanical Technology, Inc., and was appointed CEO of its fuel cell affiliate on January 1, 2014. Their fuel cell uses pure methanol as its fuel and is being considered for applications in drones and electric automobiles because of its very low specific weight. The business recently changed its name to MeOH Power.

Other business-related activities include service on the boards of several private companies, primarily in the New York Capital Region. He earlier owned the Albany "River Rats" in the American Hockey League.

Dr. Robb is a 1948 graduate of Penn State with a B.S. degree in chemical engineering. He earned M.S. (1950) and Ph.D. (1951) degrees, also in chemical engineering, from the University of Illinois.

He and his wife, Anne, celebrated their 60th wedding anniversary in 2014. They have three sons and five granddaughters, one of whom, at this writing, also is a PSU graduate and another is a student there.

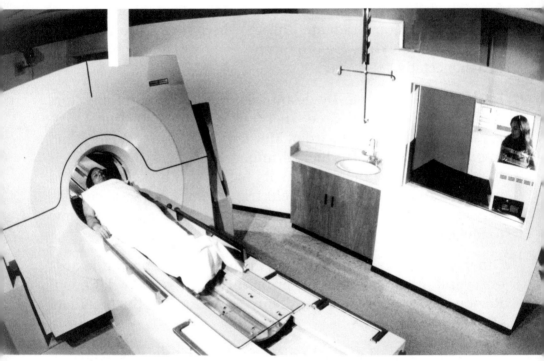

The first R & D Center 5-second CT prototype, sent to UCSF in April 1976.

INDEX OF NAMES

GENERAL INDEX